Rwanda

Beyond Wildest Imagination

Rwanda

Beyond Wildest Imagination

**Phodidas Ndamyumugabe/
Nkosiyabo Zvandasara**

Lesley Books
Berrien Springs, USA

Editor, Anne Bissell
Cover Design, Lynette Zvandasara

Ndamyumugabe, Phodidas/ Zvandasara, Nkosiyabo
Rwanda, Beyond Wildest Imagination/ Phodidas Ndamyumugabe/
Nkosiyabo Z. Zvandasara

1. Biography,   1. Title.

ISBN: 0-9660442-2-3

Dedication

This book is dedicated to all Rwandese who, in one way or another, experienced loss during the 1994 tragedy and also those that may be searching for answers to what happened in my country and may be probably wondering whether healing is ever possible.

Contents

Preface   9

Acknowledgments   11

Introduction   13

Chapter

1   Rwanda, My Home   15

2   The Drama Begins   23

3   The Rock and the Hard Place   34

4   The Unforgettable Junction   46

5   Timely Rescue   55

6   Beyond the Nyabarongo River   66

7   No Place to Hide   77

8   Bargaining With the Killers   89

9   Digging My Own Grave   101

10   When Killers Wept   111

11   Caring Killers   119

12   Ready to Die For a Tutsi   124

13   Farewell to Bush Life   137

14   Loving My Enemies   148

15   Picking the Broken Pieces   157

16   Choosing to Suffer With
      the People of Rwanda   162

Preface

It is very likely that the Rwanda genocide of 1994 may have left many people puzzled. I have also been boggled by a lot of questions about what might have gone wrong in Rwanda resulting in the killing of nearly a million people. Apart from learning about the tragedy from the media coverage of the event when it happened, I have read a few books that relate the gruesome stories, and others that try to analyze the genocide in its entirety. My attempts to understand the Rwanda tragedy seemed futile until I met one of the genocide survivors.

He was one of the new students from Rwanda on our university campus. My wife and I welcomed the opportunity to get to know Phodidas better after he paid us a visit one Saturday afternoon. We engaged in a rather general conversation with our guest but before long we realized that he had been in Rwanda during the genocide and had actually survived it.

As Phodidas related his story, he broke down several times. We gave him undivided attention knowing that letting his bottled emotions out would help him experience some sense of closure to his ordeal. We were intrigued as we listened to his thirty-six day saga of miracles upon miracles.

In toying with the idea of writing his story for the benefit of a few more people, Phodidas was encouraged by the prospect that his story might make a difference in people's understanding of the tragedy that Rwanda and its citizens had gone through. Resultant to that conviction, this book has been written. The story flows freely from Phodidas' own recollection of events and personal experiences during the genocide and is written with a prayer that it may promote healing among the people of Rwanda. It is also hoped that the book will answer a few more questions that people outside Rwanda may have had about the genocide. If in reading this story people would credit God for his miraculous survival, Phodidas believes that sharing his story may not have been in vain.

Nkosiyabo Zvandasara, D.Th., D.Min.
Adventist International Institute of Advanced Studies, Manila, Philippines.

Acknowledgments

Writing a book is rarely a solitary experience. Cognizant of that fact, I wish to extend my thanks to the individuals that assisted me in the writing of this book. Many thanks go to Pastor Daniel Opoku-Boateng, Mrs. Anne Bissell, and Mrs. Lynette Zvandasara for editing and proofreading the manuscript. I wish to also thank my friends in Rwanda for their moral support and encouragement to write my story.

Introduction

How can anyone introduce a story without preempting it? Most stories generally need no introduction. The reader is left to discover what the story is all about as it unfolds. But my story is different. I believe the reader will benefit more by being introduced to what I hope to share in this book than by leaving things to chance.

First, this book is a first hand account of what I personally experienced during the Rwanda Genocide of 1994. Much has already been said about the dark side of the Rwanda tragedy. I don't wish to overemphasize what has already been augmented. I hope that the reader will look beyond the gruesome details of the genocide and capture an alternative perspective about what really happened.

Second, no man or woman can lay claim to perfection and I am no exception. During the genocide many innocent and noble people died but I miraculously survived. Why an imperfect weakling like me miraculously survived the genocide defies all logic. Could it be that I was spared so I could tell this gripping story of my life? I leave the reader to judge.

Third, it has been a painful experience recalling what I went through. There were moments I wished to keep to myself what my eyes saw during the tragedy in my country. Indeed, to a large extent I managed to do just that during the past six years since the end of the genocide. However, two factors prompt me to share my story. First, the possible danger of remaining in a perpetual state of denial and thus depriving myself of some small measure of closure to my traumatic experiences. I hope now that a process of healing can start, no matter how difficult. Second, the prospect of offering readers an alternative perspective about what actually happened during the genocide. This should hopefully help the reader in finding a few more answers to what happened in Rwanda.

Last, I wish you God's blessing as you come with me into the drama I feel honored to testify about but would never wish to go through again. Fasten your seat belts!

Phodidas Ndamyumugabe,
Adventist International Institute of Advanced Studies,
Manila, Philippines.

♦ **(Except for my name "Phodidas Ndamyumugabe," pseudonyms have been used for all the other people's names in order to protect the innocent).**

Rwanda, My Home 1

I was born on October 3, 1970 in Kibuye, a city about 130 kilometers west of Kigali, the capital of Rwanda. My Christian parents had eight children and I was the last-born. Common to most last-born children, I felt very much pampered. I felt very much the center of my parent's love and my other siblings affectionately called me "Murusha" which means, "one who does the impossible." My fondest early childhood memories are of my parents involving me in decision making, even at the tender age of ten.

I attended Kirambo Elementary School in Kibuye for my first eight years of elementary education. In 6th Grade I was elected leader of the student body for cultural activities. On several occasions our school was in the limelight

15

and at one time the government minister for culture visited our school because of our outstanding cultural performances.

Later, I had to go to the Republic of Congo for my high school education since I could not get a place in Rwanda. Upon my arrival in Congo, I enrolled in a Catholic High School where I remained for almost two years. On account of my religious beliefs, I had to transfer to Lukanga Adventist High School where I spent the rest of my four years of high school. During the course of my stay at Lukanga, I managed to go to Rwanda on school holidays quite regularly.

In 1990, I went home to Rwanda on a long school holiday from the beginning of August to the end of September. In October, while back in school in Congo, I learned that many people had been arrested in Rwanda while others had been killed in the wake of the war between the government and the Rwanda Patriotic Front. Soon I received a letter from one of my friends in Rwanda informing me that some of my relatives had disappeared and others had been imprisoned. I longed to go back home to see my parents, but wondered if this wish was just a dream.

By the end of 1990, more and more Rwandese were becoming refugees in neighboring countries. Many young people were separated from their parents and unable to go to school. I was not only grateful to be in school, but to be in the school of my choice, Lukanga Adventist School.

In my fourth year of high school, a new law was passed in Congo requiring all foreign students to pay an examination fee of $150. This presented a challenge to me for I did not have the money. I was far from home and it was not possible for my parents to send me any money because of the war. This was a serious problem because without the money, I wasn't going to be allowed to take the final examination and therefore would not graduate from high school. One member of the staff had a desire to help me, but since he also did not have that kind of money, the only way he could assist was by encouraging me to get a Congo national ID. I rejected the idea because it was against my Christian beliefs.

As I pondered my situation, Karekezi, a Rwandese student friend offered me $100. He told me that it was money he was supposed to use to pay his boarding fees. Since my situation was urgent, in that I would not be allowed to graduate without taking the final examinations, he decided to give me the money. He moved out of the school quarters to live off campus where accommodation was cheaper and he worked to raise money for his own food which was cheaper than eating in the school's cafeteria.

Soon after my Rwandese friend had given me the $100 towards my examination fees, my roommate's mother came to visit her son Greg. Upon learning of my financial situation she gave me $50 which was the balance I needed for my examination fees. I was amazed at how kind these people had been to me.

I now had enough money to pay for the required fees and I began to prepare to write the final examinations. However, three days before the Monday I was to take the examinations, I became very ill. I had serious nose bleeding accompanied by excessive vomiting. It became obvious to me that unless God performed a miracle, I was not going to be able to sit for the examinations.

On Monday morning I woke up early and went to the examination center. I was still bleeding and had brought a handkerchief to use during the examination. However, my handkerchief got so soiled with blood that a fellow candidate offered me his to control the bleeding. It was quite a challenge for me trying to remain focused with such an inconvenience. In spite of all the problems, I passed my examinations with distinctions.

After completing my examinations I had no reason to remain at the school. I wanted to go back home to Rwanda, but I had no money. One of my sisters, who was a refugee with her husband in Congo, invited me to stay with her in her home in the City of Goma. I continued to pray and hoped that God would provide me with some money.

The following morning after completing high school, I met a pastor whom I knew very well. He informed me that he had some news for me. I wondered what it could be. He handed me a hundred dollars. He then told me that someone he had met in Rwanda had given him the money. I could not think of anybody who could have thought of me this way. Strangely, neither could the pastor recall who had given him the money. Instead of worrying much about who this person might have been, I began to thank God for answering my prayers.

Now that I had some money in my pocket, I could think of going back home in September 1992. I crossed the border safely into Rwanda and went straight to Kigali, not knowing what to expect. When I arrived in Rwanda, I met a few friends who welcomed me heartily and updated me on what had transpired during my absence. In no time at all I was part of the life of my former local church again. Soon I was elected to be one of the church elders at the tender age of 22 years old. I began to receive numerous preaching appointments in and around Kigali.

In March of 1994 I went to my village for a weekend. There I met my parents, my five sisters, and my elder brother. I was glad to see them together with all my cousins, aunts and other relatives. My visit was quite memorable because we discussed a lot of things trying to update each other on events and experiences that had occurred during the long period of separation.

I left for Kigali after the visit, with plans to return home again in July of the same year. Things were beginning to change as one politician after another began to die mysteriously. The situation in Rwanda began to deteriorate very fast after April 6, 1994 when the plane carrying the president of Rwanda, Juvenal Habyarimana, and the president of Burundi, Cyprien Ntaryamira, was shot down while returning from a peace conference in Dar es Salaam. Apparently, the two presidents had gone to Dar es Salaam to explore ways of implementing the power-sharing agreement of 1993 between the Rwandan government and the Rwandan Patriotic Front (RPF), an anti-government group which had its base in Uganda.

During this period, there was a new radio station that was spreading political propaganda. This complicated matters. Hutus were not only told to despise their Tutsi neighbors but to regard them as enemies. The messages of hate flooded the airwaves and revolutionary songs were played all day long. People were organized into political parties and the youth were trained to kill. Those who refused to join the killers were enticed by offers of a free driver's license, if they needed one, as well as other inducements. Over the radio, the youth were invited to urgent meetings that were mostly held at night.

While all this was going on, in some Christian churches the issue of Christian involvement in politics was discussed. Partisanship was discouraged while obedience to authority was encouraged. In the church, Hutus and Tutsis worked and worshipped side by side. Neighbors shared what they had and tribal distinctions were unknown to most people. Marriages between Hutus and Tutsis were common. But with widespread reports of killings, fear erupted. Relations between the two tribes deteriorated as my country tottered on the brink of imminent genocide.

I had just finished an evangelistic effort in Kicukiro School in Kigali where I had landed a teaching job in early 1993. A fellow teacher had made a decision to become a Christian following the baptism of twenty-four students. Although the number of those baptized was considerable, many students who wished to be baptized could not do so because their parents would not let them. Most of those that had been baptized, including the teacher who had been converted, later died during the genocide.

I will never forget Charles. He was one of the youth to whom I had preached. While others had been baptized, he wasn't because his father had refused. I remember talking to him prior to the baptismal service as he sobbed uncontrollably. His father simply did not want him to get baptized and all efforts by his mother to make his father understand were futile. I asked him to make a difficult decision—to choose between obeying his father or God. He was in a dilemma. He went back home and tried to convince his father one more time but in vain. After the genocide had broken out, Pierre, one of my Hutu friends informed me that he had met Charles stranded at a road-block where killers were inspecting people for ID cards. Charles told Pierre how he wished he had been baptized together with the other youth after my preaching. He also told him that his parents had been killed at the beginning of the genocide. At the end of the genocide I learned from some of my former students that Charles had been subsequently killed.

The City of Kigali was a hive of activity for it was Easter holidays and schools were closed. This gave me a chance to participate fully in church programs and I accepted an invitation to address church members on what to do in our volatile political situation. Many feared being attacked at night. After some discussions we prayed for protection as we faced a future, which was increasingly becoming uncertain.

The following Wednesday I had another appointment with a small group of businessmen. They had similar concerns over the worsening political situation. I also gave them some words of encouragement and concluded our meeting with prayer for God's will to prevail as we faced the looming crisis.

The Drama Begins 2

It was virtually impossible for anyone in the city of Kigali to go to church on the morning of April 9, 1994 because there had been a fierce gun battle in our suburb throughout the previous night. Instead of taking a risk by walking to our church building some two kilometers away, I invited to my house neighbors who were also afraid of what was going on for a prayer meeting. A handful came and by 9.00 o'clock we started our meeting.

For our meditation we selected a chapter entitled "The Time of Trouble" from the book: *Great Controversy* by Ellen G. White. We thought that this was a relevant subject taking into account our tense political situation in the country and the increasing unrest in our city. I led out in the prayer meeting. Before we prayed I drew the group's attention to the following quotation in the selected chapter:

> God's love for His children during the period of the their severest trials is as strong and tender as in the days of their sunniest prosperity; but it is needful for them to be placed in the furnace of fire; their earthliness must be consumed, that the image of Christ may be perfectly reflected. The season of distress and anguish before us will require a faith that can endure weariness, delay, and hunger—a faith that will not faint though severely tried.... Those who are unwilling to deny self, to agonize before God, to pray long and earnestly for His blessing, will not obtain it.[1]

No sooner had we started discussing the implications of the above quotation for our situation than six heavily armed militiamen entered the gate to my house. In single file, they approached my house and knocked violently. Without waiting for anyone to open the door, three stormed in and ordered us to remain seated while the other three patrolled around the house.

"IDs up!" one who appeared to be the leader of the group commanded.

Everybody promptly raised their IDs. I pretended to fumble, reached into my back pocket, and produced my citizenship permit instead. I hoped that somehow I might distract their attention. But since the permit looked different, it instantly caught the attention of the man who was standing closest to me. He snatched it from my hand, took a quick glance, and in a fit of anger sent it flying through the open door. I knew I was in deep trouble. I then quickly yet reluctantly pulled out my Tutsi ID from my shirt pocket. I handed it to him fully aware of the grim possibilities. As soon as he found out that I was Tutsi, he announced his discovery with great excitement like a prospector who has stumbled over a virgin gold mine.

"Get ready to kill!" the man shouted.

All the machetes were lifted in perfect unison awaiting the signal to cut me to pieces. For a moment I felt numb. I was now the center of all attention. Although there were other Tutsis in our prayer group, none of the militiamen showed any further interest in checking their IDs.

Then something dramatic happened. With unusual boldness, I raised my Bible and declared with unprecedented firmness, "On this ID is written Tutsi, but on my heart is written citizen of Heaven."

The commander of the militias dived for my Bible, almost losing his balance. After regaining balance he breathed heavily like a bull ready to fight. Then he began to accuse me of bragging about being a Christian.

"We don't care," he said, "Do you think that our President whom you killed wasn't a Christian too?"

He then threw my Bible to the floor and began to trample upon it with both feet in defiance. As he did so his sinister eyes surveyed me from head to toe to ensure I felt the humiliation.

Meanwhile, I became enraged as I gradually forgot my plight. I prayed in my heart saying, "Lord, I thought that you were going to protect me! Look, now even your Word is being despised. Won't you do something?"

Everyone sat frozen in fear. The machetes were still hovering over my head ready to strike. Then there was a sudden shift in focus.

"Take us to your bedroom," the commander motioned.

I stood up and led them to my bedroom. I thought he had decided to kill me away from the rest of my fellow church members. I said my last prayer and left everything in the hands of God. I was also confident that my fellow Christians would be praying for me. As we entered, two of his colleagues joined him and they scrambled for my few possessions. They looted all the pairs of shoes they could find, the only 5000 Frw (Rwanda Francs) an equivalent of US $15.00) that I had, as well as anything that they found useful. Then they brought me out of the bedroom back to the sitting room where everybody had remained. My friends were surprised to see me come back alive.

As the drama continued to unfold, I silently prayed at every breath, aware that my life could be snuffed out of me at any minute. I prayed for a miracle but also left room for God's will to be done. If God chose that I should die, I prayed that He would forgive my sins and accept me in His kingdom someday.

The commander of the militias then began to address the whole group, as I stood surrounded by the sinister-looking militiamen.

"This Tutsi is lying to you saying he is teaching you," the commander of the militias spoke as he poked me with his index finger. "You the people that killed our President. You are our enemies!"

"Why are you listening to this Tutsi? You too must be accomplices!" he alleged.

Terrified, some of my church members began to speak up. They said they did not know that I was Tutsi. Fearing for their life, some of the members of our group who were also Tutsi, but had not been discovered, claimed to be Hutu and acted surprised that I was Tutsi.

"We are not going to kill you," the commander told me. "Instead, we will call the Presidential Guard (the elite segment of the Rwanda National Army) to come and burn you alive."

The momentum to kill slackened and the machetes were lowered one after another. The commander ordered me to hand him my ID card and house keys. He thrust them into his pocket offering no explanation. I was sad to have my ID card and keys taken from me but that was nothing compared to being sliced to death by those scary machetes.

As the six militiamen walked away towards the gate one of them who was very upset with the commander's decision not to kill me immediately, sneaked from the group and headed back to me. Approaching me, he raised his knife, with all his might stabbed me twice on my head between the right ear and the top of my head. He then ran to catch up with the rest of the group. Since I had no pain whatsoever, after a while I reached for the place that had been stabbed, and to my utter amazement there was no scar, only a droplet of blood on my hair. Until now I cannot explain what happened. Apparently, God had performed yet another miracle shielding me from the stabbing that was aimed at ending my life.

After their departure we continued to pray. We thanked God for the miracles he had performed before our eyes. We entrusted our immediate future in His hands fully aware that the Presidential Guard was coming shortly to burn us alive as promised. I resumed teaching the members from the same book *The Great Controversy*, continuing with the same theme of the "Time of Trouble." But most of the members of our group could no longer concentrate on what I was teaching. They were visibly shaken by what had happened. One of the ladies suggested that instead of teaching, I should let them pray individually while awaiting the arrival of the Presidential Guard and I consented.

About an hour had passed when a young girl, possibly ten years old, knocked at the door of my house. We were scared for we did not know what to expect. The girl handed me my ID card and my house keys. What had happened was that as the six militiamen were traveling along the road they had met this small girl. They gave her instructions to bring the ID card and keys to me.

Another miracle! God had intervened and now my ID card and keys were back. We all thanked Him for this miracle.

No sooner had the young girl left for her home than the rest of my neighbors who had come for the meeting also decide to return to their respective homes. I respected their decision but urged them to continue praying. I now remained with my two friends, Jules a Hutu and Paul a Tutsi who were staying with me.

The time was now around 12.00 noon. My friends and I got out of the house in order to stretch after sitting for a long time. We had hardly walked a few meters when we saw the same militia commander, armed with a pistol and a big knife, approaching the gate of my house. We knew trouble had returned. We retreated into the house quickly, I grabbed my Bible, and we tried to escape through the backdoor over the other side of the fence. We managed to jump the fence, only to be met by a group of militias who had already encircled the house. They recognized me because they were the same militias who had been to my house a few hours ago. They ordered me to lie down on my stomach while they awaited the arrival of their commander who was coming through the front gate. In the meantime, the rest of the militias closed in on me.

Finally, the commander arrived with his furry going before him. Since I was lying on my stomach, I could not see him approach but I could hear him shouting and cursing as he came and I knew that I was about to be killed.

"I'm going to cut your throat!" he shouted as he kicked me.

Then he pulled his big knife from the sheath on his left side and lowered its pointed tip to my throat. As I felt the pressure of the knife on my throat, a strange surge of power and courage coursed through my body. I suppose this might have been my desperate desire to live. I raised my Bible, which I was firmly holding to my chest, and began to wave it, pointing it at my assailant.

"Don't spill innocent blood!" I cried.

He recoiled, removed the knife from my throat, and became agitated and crazy as if something mysterious had hit him. He threw away the knife, raised both of his hands and began to scratch the back of his head, rubbing it vigorously as if stung by a bee. He continued to mumble a lot of senseless words for an extended period of time as one who has lost his mind. All eyes were on him. His subordinates wondered what had happened to him. Amidst this confusion, I was witnessing a remarkable miracle. I believe that God had stepped in and was directly responsible for the chaos. My faith was strengthened again.

While the commander raged in his confusion, Paul and Jules sat motionless a few meters away. Nobody was saying anything to them. They were astonished and uncertain of what to expect. They remained still lest any movement would attract some attention. They were so shaken and puzzled by the difference an ID card made. Their friend (myself) was now about to be killed. What were they to do? As I look back, I believe that Jules, my Hutu friend might have been in a worse situation than my own predicament. At least I knew that soon I was going to be dead meat but he was kept in heart-wrenching suspense. For Paul, my Tutsi friend whose appearance was Hutu, his fear must have been indescribable.

After what seemed like eternity, the commander of the militias came to his senses.

"Stand up!" he ordered.

I stood up.

"If you escape after we leave this place we will conclude that you are an accomplice—go back to your house!" he commanded.

"I will never escape!" I replied quickly without paying much attention to the full scope of my words.

Yet another miracle! God had spared my life. With Paul and Jules, I returned to my house. We closed the door behind us, fell on our knees, and thanked God. We praised him for preserving our lives one more time.

At about 3.00 p.m. the same commander of the militias came back, but this time he was only passing by. I guess he was on another killing mission heading towards a destination only known to himself and his companions. This time he only called from a distance.

"Murokore, (Saint) are you in? Are you not hiding any Tutsis in there?" he inquired.

"I am around," I replied.

Here we were, defenseless but God had obviously built a wall of protection around my house. The killers could now skip my house without harming us as they combed our neighborhood for Tutsis to kill. This was very sad. We seized the opportunity to thank God for protecting us but prayed for calm to return to our troubled city.

Incidentally, I was not the only one who had been nicknamed "Murokore" I remember one Tutsi, a fellow church member who was well known in his neighborhood for his kindness. When the genocide broke out, the militias refused to touch him or his family. All militias commissioned to kill, remembered his goodness and refrained from taking his life. At one time two Tutsis, a boy aged nine and a girl aged seven, came to his home seeking refuge after their parents had been killed. He took them in. The militias pursued them all the way to his home.

When they arrived they inquired the same way as the militia commander had asked me, "Murokore, are you hiding any Tutsis?"

"No" he replied.

"All along we thought you were a saint, but now you're lying. We saw the two children come into your house!" the killers accused.

The man apologized explaining how sorry he was. He tried to reason with them insisting that even if they were the ones seeking refuge he would have hidden them the same way. He pleaded on behalf of the boy and the girl and asked the killers to spare their lives. His words fell on deaf ears.

"We will not kill you," they said. "Surrender the two children to us for we want to kill them."

He brought the poor children out and they killed the boy right before his eyes but spared the girl.

---

[1] Ellen G. White, *The Great Controversy* Mountain View, CA: Pacific Press Publishing Association, 1950, p. 621.

The Rock and the Hard Place

3

During the evening of April 13 the militias announced that nobody was to sleep in their homes that night. Everybody was to join the militias in patrolling the streets until dawn. There had been rumors of an approaching Rwanda Patriotic Front (RPF) Army. Due to my Tutsi ID, I was afraid to leave my house, but my two friends Paul and Jules decided to go. The militias made everybody line up along the road and commanded all to be vigilant. The militias wanted to use the townspeople as shields against the approaching army.

Around midnight, according to what my friends told me later, they saw a group of soldiers marching towards them. They hid among the bushes until the Rwanda Patriotic Front soldiers had walked past. Because of the full moon, my friends could tell from their hiding place that, indeed, these were the soldiers that had walked past.

After the soldiers had gone, the militias became furious. They quickly called together and addressed all the civilians they had asked to guard with them throughout the night. They told them things had changed and ordered everybody to return to their homes. They were all told to go and wait in their homes.

"Tomorrow, early in the morning, we are coming to kill all Tutsis that have not yet been killed. No one will be spared!" they emphasized.

Paul and Jules returned to my house past midnight. I asked them how things had gone but they would not say a word. Immediately, I became suspicious. I could see that their behavior was different. They appeared sorrowful and troubled. I kept on persuading them to tell me what was going on but they were tight-lipped.

After asking them, I believe the third time and without making any progress, I lashed out at them.

"Brother Jules, don't you know who I am? Do you think I will lose all hope in God now? Do you think that God will forsake me now after he has seen me through all the difficulties that I have been through?" I asked.

After my spirited speech, Jules softened. He paused and then said, "We won't hide it from you any longer. We had decided not to tell you this, but since you insisted we will now tell you. Tomorrow the militias are coming to kill you. They have made it clear that no Tutsi will be spared."

In view of what my friends had finally divulged, I remarked, "Even if the whole army comes to kill me they won't succeed unless God allows them to. I will not be killed. Let us ask God to be in charge of the situation."

We began to pray. Our prayer took a simple format. We each took turns to pray and paused for reflection at intervals. We recounted what God had already done for us in the few days that had gone by. We also turned to the Bible for encouragement and searched for God's promises that pertained to His protection and guidance. We combed the Bible for words of hope in trying times, like the one we now found ourselves in.

Although all our prayers were fervent, the one offered by Paul was particularly moving and for that reason I still remember it almost word for word.

He said, "Lord, the French government has come to rescue its citizens; the Americans have also taken away theirs, but we don't have anywhere to go. Are you not more powerful than the Americans or the French? Lord, come and save your people."

After much prayer we all became convinced that anything that was going to happen to us would be according to the will of God. We could not sleep that night because we did not want to be attacked unprepared. At dawn as I was sitting on my bed meditating on several passages of scripture that deal with God's protection, something happened. I heard a shout. Someone was hitting our gate very hard. The person was calling with a shrill in his voice, asking us to open for him.

"Open!" he continued to shout.

I woke my friends up. We all thought that the militias had come according to the threat they had made the previous night. Thinking that I was the target, I decided not to answer.

One of my friends responded instead.

"I will open for you!" he shouted.

But my friend was so shaken that he could not take even one step. As a result, he continued to delay and didn't go to open the gate. Meanwhile, I was busy praying asking God to place an angel by our gate so that nobody would come and harm us.

Then suddenly there was a big bang. A heavy explosion occurred right close to my house. Immediately it became quiet. The shouting ceased. Up to today, I don't know what exactly happened. All I know is that the militias did not come. Again, God had extended his protection over us.

We had been spared and were grateful for it but another drama was quickly unfolding. After sunrise we saw many people from the surrounding suburbs converging on our suburb. It was very obvious that they were running away from the areas where fighting seemed fiercest. A large number of people came in search of refuge and found an empty high-rise building not far from my house. As it turned out, that building was no refuge at all because people from there were killed ruthlessly. From my house I could see them killed by being thrown down the steps or thrown from the windows from several floors up. Those who were not completely dead by the time they hit the ground were sliced up by the militia's machetes that they brandished as they stood at the foot of the building.

In an effort to escape the killing, many tried to run to my house. People were desperate looking for somewhere to hide. I saw close to my house two small children aged about five and seven years respectively. They also rushed to my house seeking shelter and they told me that both of their parents had been killed the previous day. My house soon became full and many people spilled out into the yard. As a result, my house became a target for the militias.

In the wake of this influx, we thought of fleeing to another district. I considered the option but realized that my Tutsi ID card would complicate things for me. I needed a Hutu ID card to escape. Jules asked me to tear up my Tutsi card, but I refused. I insisted that I would not lie by disguising my identity and saying that I am a Hutu. I declared that it was God who had saved me in the past and not an ID card or any ingenuity on my part. I decided that

I would rather die honest that lie in order to live. I kept my Tutsi ID and asked my friends to pray.

Meanwhile, Pierre, my other Hutu friend, who stayed in the same suburb of Kigali arrived accompanied by his younger brother, Samson. We were happy to see them. They brought us a cake that we ate quickly and were grateful for the energy it provided us for we had not eaten any food for two days. Pierre suggested we leave Kigali and flee south to Gitarama District, or somewhere outside Kigali where it would be peaceful. We did not know exactly to which part of Gitarama we were headed to, but we all felt convinced that leaving Kigali was the only option we had.

Unbeknown to me, Pierre had devised a plan that would facilitate my safe passage through the City of Kigali, since going to Gitarama entailed cutting through Kigali. He asked for my ID card and placed it under his. The strategy was that if anyone would ask us to produce our IDs Pierre would go first, show his Hutu ID then when my turn came, Pierre would say he had my card and would come back and show them his ID card. He rationalized that since our ID cards were back to back with Pierre's Hutu card on top of mine that would not amount to dishonesty. Besides, if the militias decided to search us, they would not find any card on me since Pierre had both cards.

Due to the pressure of the moment, I did not weigh the ethical implications of Pierre's intentions. I packed a few of my belongings, which consisted of a few books, a big portable radio, and some clothes. One of my friends carried the books and I took the radio since it was heavier. Now there were five of us—Pierre, Samson, Paul, Jules, and myself.

We were ready to start on our long journey that was to take us across Kigali through numerous roadblocks. We left Kigali on Friday, April 15 around 9.00 o'clock in the morning. The journey was long not because of the distance, but because of the amount of roadblocks and the numerous events that crowded our journey. At each of these roadblocks and even in between them, were sporadic ID card checks by the militias who were bent on eliminating anyone bearing a card written "Tutsi."

As we left my house it dawned on us that there was nowhere to hide. Around us were people being killed because they did not have IDs written "Hutu." As I looked some fifty meters ahead of us, I saw dead and dying people piled on either side of the road with many others scattered all over. Some people were drenched in blood screaming for help, but the militias seemed to continue brutalities without any mercy. At one time we thought of returning to my house, but even back there, people were being killed like flies. The only option was to advance for retreat would spell death, and to linger would court the wrath of the already angry militias.

Meanwhile, I was praying in my heart that God would help us pass this first roadblock safely. Instead of entertaining more horrific scenes of what might lie ahead, I decided to take one step at a time. My prayer was specific and focused on the roadblock right before my eyes. Pierre used his strategy. He approached the killer who wanted to see the ID and seeing that it was written Hutu he let him pass and then asked me to produce mine. Immediately, Pierre told the militiaman, "I have his card!" He then came back and just flashed it. The militiaman did not even read it but signaled to let me pass through. I had been spared. As I walked past, I recognized some of the people who had been ordered to sit down. They were waiting to be killed. My heart sank in terror.

Paul was detained at this very roadblock and made to stand among those about to be killed. Pierre decided to go back and try to negotiate the release of Paul leaving me to continue with Jules and Samson. What had happened was that on April 6, after the death of the President had been announced, Paul quickly decided to tear his Tutsi ID card up because many Tutsis were being killed. This is why he could not go through the roadblock. They wanted him to produce an ID but he had none. Sadly we had to leave him there. There was nothing anyone of us could do to help our friend. However, we prayed that Pierre would somehow secure the release of Paul.

Hardly fifty meters down the road, Jules, Samson, and I came to another roadblock. I should point out that it was very difficult to continue without Pierre who had helped me pass through the previous roadblock. At the previous roadblock where he had decided to remain negotiating Paul's release, he had handed me my ID card. As we proceeded, the many dead people we saw on either side of the road increasingly appalled us. Then as we approached the militias I pleaded with God.

"Lord close their eyes!"

Just as we came to where the militias were, a car full of people pulled up. All the attention of the militias manning the roadblock shifted to the people in the car leaving me to pass unnoticed. God had done it again! We thanked Him for another safe passage.

Although we had reason to celebrate, the ordeal was far from over because just after passing the roadblock we saw another militiaman leaning on a street pole. He was smoking something that I suspect must have been marijuana because it did not look like a kind of cigarette I had seen before. I knew that he too would want to see my ID card. Instantly, I whispered a prayer—the same prayer, "Lord, close his eyes and let me pass" When I got to him he asked me for my ID card. I gave it to him. As he tried to open my ID his hands were shaking uncontrollably like someone with severe Parkinson's disease. He kept struggling to open my ID while looking at my face.

"Don't you communicate with these rebels?" he asked.

"No!" I replied.

He handed my ID card back and Samson, Jules, and I proceeded on. Another miracle had taken place and we thanked God for closing the eyes of this militiaman.

Another fifty meters, and this time it was not the usual roadblock, just a chaotic group of people blocking the road. Many were asking for IDs and many were busy producing them and there was so much commotion. I knew they were going to require me to also produce my ID. Jules did not have a problem because he had a Hutu ID and Samson was too young to have one, so no one ever bothered him. Again I prayed the same prayer asking God to close their eyes so I could pass as I had done before. When we got to the place, I took advantage of the chaos. I sneaked through the crowd as if my ID had already been checked. Because everyone seemed so busy, I managed to go through yet another obstacle as I strove to get to the other side of Kigali.

The series of roadblocks were far from over, hardly another fifty meters down the road I came to yet another roadblock. Confident that God would not let me down, I prayed: "Close their eyes!" But the first person to see me asked for my ID and I gave it to him. When he saw that my features were Tutsi he whispered: "Are you Tutsi?

Disappear!" He quickly handed me my card and I walked past. I didn't run for that would have aroused much suspicion. Again God had answered my prayer! I had thought that the answer to my prayer was going to lie in the militiaman's failure to detect my Tutsi features, but God chose to answer my prayer another way. He doesn't run out of options! This was the fifth formal roadblock that I had gone through with no problem.

We were getting tired and we were not even halfway across Kigali, but we had to move on. There was no way we could stop and rest. As we approached the next militiaman, he asked us: "Why are you traveling on foot? Wait here I will get you a ride!" Fortunately, he did not ask for our ID cards. In no time he stopped a small pick-up truck, but the driver looked fiercer that the man who had offered to secure us a ride. He agreed to pick us up only after being threatened by the militiaman that if he were not going to give us a ride he would not leave. We were forced into the truck as one of the militiamen confirmed our IDs had been checked by asking,

"Are your IDs checked?"

"Yes!" we said in unison.

Then we jumped on the small pick-up truck.

As soon as we got into the truck, the driver diverted from the main road and began driving towards Kiyovu. Our brief ride on the truck was far from comfortable because after traveling for a kilometer, the truck stopped.

The driver came to the back where we were sitting. He pulled out a strange-looking machete—two pronged and double-edged. I wondered what next.

"Why did you get onto my truck?" the man asked sounding very confused.

For a moment I thought he was going to kill us. Then he shouted, "Everybody, everybody, I'm going to give all of you guns so we may go out and kill!"

Then he quickly changed his mind. "Everyone, off my truck, I don't want to see you!" he said.

Puzzled about what was going on, yet thankful to God, we made our way back to the main road as we watched his truck fade into the distance.

Before we reached the main road, we met a group of Congolese walking in the opposite direction. They were speaking in Swahili. Having lived in Congo for more than six years, I was able to tell from their features that they were not Rwandese. I asked them where they were going. They gave me not only a cold but also a very rude response.

"Sisi tuna kwenda kuEmbassy yetu!" (We are going to our embassy), they replied. They clearly showed they did not want anything to do with me. When we saw them come, we had thought of joining their group. But now it was clear that they did not wish to associate with us, and so we let them go by as we proceeded to the junction where the truck had turned towards Kiyovu.

The Unforgettable Junction 4

With each step that Jules, Samson, and I took towards the main junction in Kigali, hope was waning. I began to doubt whether God would repeat the same miracles that He had already performed throughout the roadblocks we had successfully passed thus far. I was utterly confused and a fierce tug of war was raging in my heart. Which way were we to go? Should we retrace our steps and go back to the main road we had come on or perhaps go forward through Kigali to the other side? We vacillated. We looked to the right and to the left and only saw roadblocks with people being killed. We lingered momentarily, but to do so seemed just as dangerous as proceeding.

I then invited my friends to pray with me. This time we huddled together the way basketball players do during decisive time-outs during championship games. Our prayer was pithy and to the point. I prayed, "Lord, lead us. Tell us where to go from here."

Instantly, we felt a conviction to proceed with our arduous journey.

Not too long after we were overjoyed when Pierre and Paul caught up with us. The last we had seen them was when we had left Paul detained at one of the roadblocks when he had failed to produce any ID card because he had torn his card up before we started on our journey through Kigali. Somehow, Pierre had managed to remain with him negotiating for his release, fully aware of the risk involved. Miraculously, they had made it to where we were. Upon seeing me, Pierre and Paul were so surprised because they thought they had seen my body among some of the dead along the road. With tears in their eyes they praised God that we could be reunited and we were alive.

Together we continued to the next roadblock just before the main traffic circle or roundabout in the center of Kigali. Those people inspecting ID cards seemed equally ferocious as the ones we had met along the way. It seemed that more trouble was waiting for us.

"Lord, close their eyes!" I prayed.

God did not seem to close anybody's eyes this time because as soon as I got there one militiaman asked for my ID card. I gave it to him. Upon reading "Tutsi", the man shouted: "We have found one!"

Instantly, a group of fierce-looking men armed with bloodstained machetes converged around me. My other friends, Jules and Samson, continued on their way, including Paul who though Tutsi, had fooled many by his Hutu features. Pierre my Hutu friend remained with me, pleading for my release. He tried all he could, even offering them some money. But nothing seemed to soften any of their hearts. In fact, the more he begged for my release, the more irritated they became.

"You are an accomplice!" one of the men shouted angrily at Pierre.

Another militiaman could not take it any more and he charged towards Pierre, but agile Pierre fled. The man chased after him, but Pierre outran him. Frustrated, he returned. Pierre had escaped a machete that was going to kill him.

After they had engulfed me, my fate took a nasty turn. One of the militias ordered me to go and lie among the dead, right next to one man they had recently killed and who was still bleeding profusely. I would not lie down. I did not want to die. Adamant, I refused to lie down and stood still.

I began to pray. I said, "Lord, time has come for you to show your protection. Show them that I am your servant and that you are my God!"

I waited for what seemed to be an eternity. I was forgotten. All of the militiamen were caught up with the increasing traffic of cars and people coming to the roadblock. I was afraid but patient. I took advantage of the delay to pray even more passionately. The odds were clearly against me.

Then, one of the militias looked in my direction.

"We didn't kill that man!" he shouted loud enough for everyone to hear.

In furry, he ran in my direction, brandishing his machete, coming to kill. As he approached I squeezed in a short prayer.

"Lord, stop him in Jesus' name!" I prayed.

The man walked briskly towards me and raised his machete ready to strike me down. I prayed with my eyes wide open. Then something dramatic took place. When he was about one meter from where I was standing, he made a sudden U-turn. It seemed as if something or someone had prevented him from getting close to me. He walked back to where he had come from, across to the other side of the road. He seemed confused. I remained standing and untouched, but also wondering what had happened to stop him.

God had decided to answer my prayer in a miraculous manner. I believe that God had sent his angel to protect me. Given the fury with which the man had charged towards me, the only explanation I had for what I saw was that God had directly intervened to guarantee my safety at that critical moment.

Time elapsed and I remained among the dead not knowing what to expect. Everybody seemed caught up with searching IDs at the roadblock. I saw many people come to the roadblock. Some made it through while others were trapped and consigned to die. While sympathetic with those that appeared stranded, I felt very much stranded myself.

Another militiaman observed that I was still alive and yet the order had already been given that I must be killed. He shouted pointing in my direction.

"That man is not yet killed!" he complained. "What's going on here?"

Upset by what he considered sheer dereliction of urgent duty, he took it upon himself to come kill me as soon as he could. He began to run towards me, his feet barely touching the ground, and I knew this was the end of my life.

"Lord, stop him in Jesus' name!" I repeated the same prayer.

I knew that I was totally defenseless and that my only hope was in God. I saw the man raise his machete, ready to strike! But when he came just a meter from where I was standing, he suddenly stopped and in a split second made an about turn. He too retraced his steps all the way across the road to where he had come from.

Talk of miracles! I was grateful to witness God at work. I thought I was dreaming, but I wasn't. It was real. I was part of the drama and God was in charge.

By now my confidence in God was strengthened. I knew God would take care of me no matter what happened. To be honest, I also felt a certain degree of numbness—some sort of resignation. I had been through a lot and had realized that panic was a waste of time. I was prepared for the worst. But God was far from deserting me.

Another ten or so minutes passed and I was still standing awaiting my fate. A third militiaman saw me and remarked the same way the other two had done before.

"Why are we not killing that man," he also complained. "I will go and do it myself!"

He approached me boiling with anger and wielding his bloodthirsty machete. He seemed determined to wipe me out of existence.

"Lord, stop him in Jesus' name!" I prayed that short prayer which had worked miracles before.

But unlike the other two killers before him, this one came all the way, right to my nose.

"What has happened to that protection which had insulated me from the first two militias?" I wondered to myself.

His machete pointing to the ground, the man looked me in the eye, studying my face with unquestionable thoroughness. The man's fury had instantly cooled down. Undoubtedly, his burning temper had melted into a mixture of tameness and wonderment.

"Uri muntu ki? (By the way, what kind of person are you?)" He asked.

"I am a man of God. I am a preacher!" I replied with much confidence.

In a subdued voice he suggested, "I will go fetch your ID card."

I welcomed the prospect of getting my ID card back after it had been confiscated. After a while, he came back with the news that they had refused to release my card.

"Don't you have any money to give those guys so they may give your card back and let you go?" he asked.

"I don't have any money on me," I responded.

"I'm sorry," he spoke with much regret. "There is nothing more I can do to help you."

All along I had been standing on the island of the roundabout, the part around which cars encircle, with dead people lying all around me. Across the road, perhaps some twenty meters away from the roadblock where the checking of IDs was taking place sat another man armed with a gun. From the amount of authority he seemed to wield, I concluded that he might have been one of the leaders of the group of militias. He instructed one of the juniors to call me. I made my way across the road to where this "leader" was. For some reason he didn't talk to me. I stood before him and waited for anything to happen.

I wondered why he had called me in the first place if he did not want to talk to me. I wasn't about to complain since coming across the road gave me a chance to stretch after being stuck in one place for a long time.

Meanwhile, another man came to me. I was able to recognize him for he was the same man who had come to me while I was standing among the dead determined to kill me after the other two had failed. He was the same man who had ended up offering to negotiate for the release of my ID card but had been unsuccessful.

"Did you say that you're a man of God?" he asked.

"Yes!" I responded.

"If you're a man of God, why don't you go and ask for your ID card?" he spoke with great authority.

At that moment a strange feeling came over me. My strength was revived. Great courage filled my heart. The words this man spoke sounded as if spoken by an angel. I instantly remembered the way I had recently prayed in Jesus' name and militias had failed to destroy me. I was convinced that if I would command them in Jesus' name they would give me back my ID card and let me go.

Fired up by this boldness, I made my way towards the militiamen who had kept my ID card. I had only made a few steps when that man whom I described as the leader, the man who had called me from across the island of the roundabout, the man who had left me to stand beside him while he remained mute, suddenly came back to life.

"Give him his ID card!" he commanded in a loud voice.

I proceeded to the militiamen who seemed puzzled as they handed me my ID card.

"What kind of bribe did you give to our boss?" they inquired.

"Nothing!" I replied.

After getting my card, the same man who had said, "If you're a man of God, why don't you go and ask for your ID card" instructed me saying, "Go! But...." He didn't complete the sentence.

I left the roundabout. Walking a few meters downhill, I caught up with my friends who were sitting besides the road without knowing whether to continue or not. They were so discouraged for they thought that I had already been killed. They never thought that they would see me again. My friends were very happy and surprised to see me alive and well. Again God had performed a series of mind-boggling miracles in a compressed space of time.

Timely Rescue 5

After reuniting with Pierre and Paul who had been detained at one of the roadblocks, Samson and Jules and I were glad to have come this far safely, although we clearly knew that our problems were far from over. We reminded ourselves how God had delivered us from the many dangerous situations and were convinced that we owed our being alive to God alone and not to chance or human ingenuity. As we continued on our difficult journey, we came to another group of people who seemed confused and afraid not knowing whether to proceed to the next roadblock or retreat. From afar we could see that the next roadblock was fearsome.

Before getting to the next roadblock we came to a kiosk just a few meters down the road. What came to mind was not buying some food but praying. We decided to pray behind the kiosk because it seemed convenient and not too suspicious.

It was a memorable occasion. Although there was no time to kneel for prayer, we all took turns to pray audibly. We opened our hearts in thankfulness to God for the protection He had given us. We wept. We renewed our commitment to God and entrusted our lives to His care.

We made our way back to the main road. No sooner had we come back to the main road than Pierre my Hutu friend, complained about my ID card again. He knew all the havoc my Tutsi ID card had caused, so he insisted that I tear it. We slowed down and then stopped. I became confused, but quickly regained my emotional bearings. How would I help him appreciate my conviction?

"Do you still have the card?" he inquired with unmistakable anger simmering on his face.

"You know where I stand already," I explained. "I don't want to depend on myself. I would rather have God defend me the way He has been doing so far, than to take matters into my own hands under such dangerous circumstances."

I argued that tearing my card would signal my lack of trust in God's ability to fully protect me. I did not want to be presumptuous. Neither did I wish to lie by denying my Tutsi identity. I was confident that God would not let me down. I was convinced that my basis for action was one of faith rather than presumption.

"If you have faith in God's presence and protection, then let us proceed!" said Pierre after understanding my position.

After my speech, everybody, particularly Pierre, became convinced that we could go on without destroying my Tutsi ID card. We took up our belongings and continued on our journey.

As we approached another roadblock our fears intensified. We heard stories of how people were being killed and thrown into the Nyabarongo River—the same river that we intended to cross on our way to Gitarama. Our fears grew even worse when we came to the roadblock that seemed far more bloody and wicked than the ones we had seen before. Women, men, and children were being killed mercilessly. Another cluster of militiamen was sitting on the left side of the road and watching with fiendish delight. To say it was scary is an understatement.

Jules became very frightened and could no longer conceal it. He almost fainted from the horrors of the bloodshed. His knees were so shaky; he stumbled and almost fell to the ground. That attracted the attention of the militias. They beckoned him to come to where they were sitting.

"What's going on?" one of the man inquired with a voice full of sarcasm.

"These are the people we're looking for. Come here!" they shouted in one voice.

Jules was detained at this roadblock for questioning. The rest of us continued without being stopped. In retrospect, this was another miracle because when Jules stumbled that distracted the killers and reduced the chances of my being asked for an ID card. This was a blessing in disguise because his stumbling prevented the militias from asking all of us to produce our IDs. When they began to concentrate on Jules, my Hutu friend, we knew he could produce his ID card and there would be no problem.

Along the way, we met many people that we were able to recognize. Some rich and prosperous Tutsis we knew very well were in trouble. Between the previous roadblock and the next we managed to talk to one Tutsi businessman who was perhaps in his late twenties. His business had been robbed, pruning him of everything he owned and now he was frantically trying to escape the militias who had killed some of his family members. I could see that he was desperate, terrified, and confused. We persuaded him to come with us to Gitarama where we were headed.

"The Lord will protect us!" I assured him.

"I have never prayed before," he confessed. "Do you think that God will protect me?" he wondered.

"I have never prayed in all my life! How can I start now?" the rich man continued to protest.

He refused to come with us. This did not disturb me much since we also did not know whether where we were headed was any better than where we had come from. What bothered me most, however, was his refusal to pray to God. My heart ached as I thought of his predicament. True, we all were in trouble; we all had things taken from us by force; we all had fled our homes for safety; we all were being hunted, and had had close relatives killed. Yet, for a moment I forgot my plight and focused on his. I felt sorry for him because he had nowhere to turn and when I offered him God for an option he lacked interest.

Although things were far from normal, my friends and I had a God in whom we could place our trust in such difficult times. God had already given us persuasive and concrete glimpses of his power through the miracles he had already performed since the beginning of the genocide. We longed to share with many hopeless people that came our way this unfailing security we had found in God which we had proven firsthand.

From this point until we crossed over to Gitarama, there were no formal roadblocks any more. Instead, every inch of the way became a roadblock because of the indiscriminate inspection of ID cards that was taking place. The entire road was a hive of activity, reminiscent of an open-air market at its peak. There was so much killing and chaos. Although all the phases of our journey had been infested with danger, this part seemed the most dangerous. What made it more treacherous was the fact that the sun had gone down and it was turning dark. The darker it grew it seemed the more ruthless the militias became.

I had noticed earlier that on both sides of the road were lorries that were carrying bodies. Apparently, prisoners had been brought along to load those who had been killed into the trucks. I saw gut-wrenching atrocities. More people than I could number lay dead or half-dead.

It seemed to me that the urge to kill was so strong that the militias were either getting too tired, or more and more ruthless. Many had been struck by an axe on the side of the head in front of the ear only once and had been left to die slowly. Countless people were writhing in pain, wallowing in their own blood inside the trucks. With more people being added on top of the already full trucks, the victims cried as they raised their heads and threw their legs and arms in the air.

Many opted to be killed faster, but no militiaman seemed kind enough to give anyone a less brutal death. In spite of the chaos, the militias had a well-organized and systematic way of killing. One group of militias formed a line that blocked the road. Anyone in this group of militias would ask for IDs. Whenever they came across a Tutsi, he or she would be directed to a man who sat off the side of the road axing the victims one by one as they came.

In all this confusion I lost contact with Paul, my Tutsi friend who had earlier torn his I. D. card up for fear of being killed. Progress on this part of our journey was very slow. It took us three hours to cover about half a kilometer.

As I squeezed through the thick traffic, I came to a group of men armed with machetes. They were directing people, one after another without asking for IDs, to a designated place where militias waited, axes in hand, ready to kill all possessing Tutsi ID cards. I was directed to the man who sat about seven meters away. I quickly mastered the procedure from those that went before me. They would walk close to him; flash their cards at him; he would lean forward to check whether the card read Hutu or Tutsi; if Hutu he would let the person pass; but if Tutsi, he would then lean backwards and swing his axe. I saw no trace of pity on his face. I braced up for the execution by offering a simple and straightforward prayer.

"Lord, that man is ferocious and doesn't have pity. If he gets angry, you must also get angry, Oh Lord!" I prayed earnestly.

Just as I lifted my leg to take the final step to flash my card to the militiaman who sat ready to perform his bloody duty, I was violently grabbed by the collar from the back. I froze.

"Where are you going?" Jules who had been detained at the previous roadblock after stumbling had caught up with us just in time to grab me by the collar thus saving me from execution.

"I'm going to show that man my ID card." I replied.

"There is a car waiting for you hurry up!" he urged.

I went the opposite direction and averted what might have spelt my end. As I looked on the other side of the road, sure enough there was a car waiting for me. But before I could cross over to where the car was parked, Jules, my friend who had whisked me from imminent danger absorbed a few stinging words from one of the militias.

"Why are you taking him away? The man asked with furry.

"Let him go to the car because even after he boards the car, he will pass through this way anyway!" he persuasively argued.

"Since you will come through here, I will let you go!" the militiaman agreed.

I hopped into the small truck. Unfortunately the truck would not start. We jumped off the truck and tried to push-start it. It coughed and then responded after a short while. I was glad that nobody had asked me anything—not even my ID card! However, the truck was overloaded with lots of luggage and people. In fact, some tried to bury themselves under the luggage to escape the searching eyes of the militias. As soon as I got onto the truck, I also tried to squeeze under the bags, but it was useless. I couldn't shrink in size. I then decided to sit on the luggage instead. I continued to remind myself of God's unfailing protection.

Lost in thought, my momentary peace was quickly interrupted by two men who came and pulled away one passenger who was sitting right beside me. I don't know why they chose him. There seemed to be nothing spectacular about him. If this was sheer randomness, how safe was I on this truck, I wondered. They threw him into a lorry that was parked close by and he landed on top of dead bodies. The truck drove off. After a while, the man came back safe and he joined the rest of the group.

I was glad that Jules had pulled me on the spur of the moment from being killed by the ax man. It was important to remember that he had been detained at the roadblock after he stumbled, unable to stand the gruesome killings. Providentially, God sent him to whisk me from danger at the last moment. God had performed another miracle! I praised him for such a timely rescue. Prayer and more prayer was all I could offer for every second seemed full of indescribable danger. I had every reason to thank God for past deliverance. I also took the opportunity to ask him to protect me in the present as well as the future.

Tension mounted as we rode along wondering what the next stop had in store for us. We came to a place where we were ordered to get off the truck. There was another impromptu inspection of ID cards. A young man approached me and asked for my ID card. I reluctantly handed him my card. He read it and saw that I was Tutsi.

"I'm going to shout for everyone to know who you are," he whispered.

His voice sounded like someone who was expecting to be bribed. Pierre picked up the clue and began to negotiate with the man for my release. At one point it seemed that Pierre had miscalculated because the man became so adamant. He was not going to let me go. Although he had threatened to kill me, somehow he also seemed to be buying time. He continued to send mixed messages leaving Pierre to believe that there was room still for bargaining. I prayed as the "talks" dragged. Pierre was not about to give up. Finally, when Pierre offered him 300 Francs and my radio, the man released me. Although I had vowed to remain honest and not help God, my humanity got the best part of me. I had inadvertently "helped" God.

We were cheered to see that all the way to the Nyabarongo River—the river separating Kigali from Gitarama, there were no more roadblocks. "Free at last!" we each echoed and re-echoed. Our crossing the river reminded me of the story of the children of Israel crossing the Red Sea. There was rejoicing. We broke into songs of deliverance and joy.

This still was April 15, 1994, the same day we had left Kigali. But April 15 was also six days after we had been attacked on Saturday April 9 while praying in my house.

Across the Nyabarongo River killings were yet unknown. In this part of the country, life was still normal. We had a great deal of time to reflect on the miracles God had done for us. We had crossed our Jordan, passing from death to life. We later paused to eat the cake that Pierre had packed into his bag before leaving my house—the cake had been long forgotten because of the strenuous demands of our journey through Kigali. For the first time in a week we could eat, lie down on the ground, and enjoy a long and uninterrupted sleep.

Beyond the
Nyabarongo River

6

Friday evening, April 15, was very peaceful in contrast to all that we had gone through that day, since the beginning of our journey from Kigali. Here in Gitarama district, the other side of the Nyabarongo River, people were still human. Here peace still reigned supreme. Only occasional rumors of the genocide in Kigali tarnished the calmness. As we reminisced on our painful ordeal, we all wondered how base people in Kigali had become.

On our way to Pierre's home we met one of the militiamen that had come to my house that Saturday in Kigali. I immediately recognized him. He was part of the group that had come to my house and looted everything I had. I drew close to him and this time I was not afraid because he was on crutches limping and had no machete in hand.

He did not seem to recognize me and if he did, he preferred not to show it. He might have had a fear that we
would harm him. I quickly noticed that the shoes he was
wearing were mine—the shoes he had taken from me by
force at my house. My friends also recognized him.

"Why are you on crutches," I asked. "What happened
to you?"

He told us that he had been shot in the leg in a fierce
clash in Kigali in which many of his friends had been
killed. He, however, managed to escape and cross the Nyabarongo River to Gitarama.

This seemed like a perfect time for revenge. He was
vulnerable. We could now teach him a few lessons. My
friends insisted that he give back all the things he and his
fellow militias had stolen from my house.

"Leave him in peace!" I pleaded.

My friends were very responsive to my plea and no
one touched him. I then asked him to exchange the shoes
with me that he had stolen for the ones I was wearing. I
preferred the ones he had on because they were more
comfortable and stronger.

"Please, let me keep the shoes," he begged. "I'm sorry
for what I did."

I doubted whether he really was sorry for what he did
or perhaps he was only sorry that he had been discovered.
Giving it a second thought, I realized that he was not the
basic problem. This militiaman had been used by the devil

that was the real culprit behind all the evil filling our land. I felt sorry for him and decided to forgive him. We let him go unharmed.

We continued on our way to Pierre's home where we expected to meet his family. As we traveled, Pierre dreamed aloud of how he hoped to help me in Gitarama. He told me that I was to forget about Kigali and its problems for he was going to help me find a job. He reminded me of how God had been so good to us and pledged that he was going to do everything in his power to make me comfortable and settled.

We finally arrived at Pierre's home, Saturday afternoon, April 16 tired but glad to be home. His parents, whom I had never met, welcomed us and took me in as their child. We told of our ordeal and Pierre's parents listened with horror, then they praised God that we had made it safely. We ate the first decent meal we had had in days after which we went to bed and enjoyed a peaceful sleep.

Early Sunday morning we went to church. In most parts of Rwanda many Christians go to church four times a week—Saturday, Sunday, Wednesday, and Friday. Wednesday is mid-week prayer meeting and Friday evening is another meeting. On Saturday, some Christians meet for worship services, but on Sundays some go to church to hold other special services. Sunday is a day when people bring their tithes and offerings to church.

This is also the day when people come to perform different chores for the up-keep of the church building. There was a brief worship service that Sunday and we gladly participated, in fact, they asked me to give a short testimony. I agreed and shared some of the miracles God had worked in our lives during the previous week.

After the service, the leader of the church asked me to preach to them again the following Saturday. I accepted, and then we returned to my friend's home. Monday and Tuesday were uneventful.

Wednesday, April 20, Pierre, Samson, Paul and I went to attend mid-week prayer meeting. I was invited to give more testimony and was surprised by the overwhelming attendance. I inquired whether this was the trend. They informed me that many had come to hear me speak because they had heard about my preaching through friends and relatives before my coming to Gitarama. This was because I used to conduct evangelistic meetings in Kigali and some of the surrounding communities.

Soon after arriving at Pierre's home, Jules decided to visit his family in Ntongwe *Commune* (settlement), 20 kilometers East of Ruhango where we were. I remained with Pierre's family. After a few days, Jules returned and asked whether I could come with him to his home. I agreed. Jules' parents were glad to see me and I quickly felt at home. The cordial treatment I received at my friends' homes, Pierre and Jules though both were Hutu, was incredible. Again, I was asked to preach during their Wednesday prayer meeting.

We were enjoying peace and only heard about killings in neighboring *communes*. If I had known the future, I would have fled to the Republic of Burundi nearby, but it was too late.

On Thursday, twenty-four years old Claudette and her fifteen-year-old brother Joel came to Jules' home. These siblings were seeking refuge after fleeing from the southern part of Ntongwe *Commune*, after their village had been attacked. They told how people were being killed and confirmed rumors we had heard earlier that the primary targets of the militias were the rich, the educated Hutu, and any Tutsi. This meant that Jules and his sister Jemime, who were well educated and Hutu, together with Claudette and Joel (the two refugees from Ntongwe), and myself were in the same predicament. News kept on coming and it became apparent that a group of militias was closing in on us. Jules and I knew how ruthless the militias could be. This was terrifying.

The killings in Ntongwe were triggered by the visit of the new President who had recently been installed to take the place of the President killed in the plane crash. In his speech while visiting the Butare *Prefecture* (district), a place about 130 kilometers South of Kigali, he had stated in no uncertain terms that in all *prefectures* killing should start. All Hutus who chose to be neutral were to be killed together with all the Tutsis.

It was not easy. Any Hutu who would not kill had to be killed, and those Hutus who hid Tutsis were putting their own lives at risk. There was no neutrality. Hutus were forced to kill Tutsis and any of their own tribe who would not cooperate in the killings. There were moments when I thought that being Tutsi was preferable than being Hutu—as a Tutsi I knew my fate, but many Hutus who were Christian or had morals, found themselves in a dilemma because they were forced to kill against their will.

During my stay at Jules' home I had a bit of time to reflect on what was going on in my country. Since I was caught in the heat of the tragedy, I tried to grasp what was happening. I was disturbed to see how people who had been good neighbors and devout Christians were converted into killers.

For anyone to understand how this could happen, one needs to know that there were basically four groups of people among those that participated in the genocide. The first group was made up of Hutu extremists. These were loyal to Hutu political parties and were steeped in tribalism. Some might have harbored chronic feelings of resentment against the Tutsis and were looking for any opportunity to kill. Since those who harbored ill feelings were a minority, they tried to involve as many people as possible. Otherwise many Rwandese were unconscious of the ethnic differences.

The second group was that of hooligans, thieves, and robbers. These may have been drawn into killing the Tutsis because they wanted to plunder the property of the victims of the genocide. Most of these people may have been in it for material gain and not for any other reason. They may have seen this as an opportunity to line their pockets with money and enrich themselves from the things the Tutsis and some rich targeted Hutus had acquired through toil.

The third group consisted of those that had been deceived. The militias polarized the Hutus against their Tutsi neighbors. They produced forged documents and signed papers showing that their Tutsi neighbors were collaborating with rebels. People that had lived in harmony with each other were taught to hate each other. There were cases where the politicians would tell Hutus that the pits that their Tutsi neighbors had dug were not toilets or latrine holes but were graves where they intended to bury Hutus as soon as the Tutsi Army invaded the country. All those that believed the militias began to join their ranks. Neighbor was turned against neighbor.

The fourth group was made up of the timid. There were many that became killers because they were afraid of being killed themselves. This may be where the majority of Christians, the kind-hearted, and those with morals found themselves. They may not have wanted to kill but they were forced against their will and ended up killing. This was a time of sifting.

I have spoken to, and heard many people outside Rwanda, such as international organizations, scholars, theologians, and historians, among others, ask, "What went wrong in Rwanda? How is it that in a country such as Rwanda with so many Christians a genocide could happen?"

These questions continue to be asked. Yet an insight into what was happening will clear much of the mist. Let me share with you one story that took place. One Hutu Christian was forced to be part of the killing in Gitarama District. They took him to a roadblock where they were going to stop and kill all the Tutsis they could find. As soon as they came to the point where they were going to start their business, they discovered that this Christian stood passively without killing like everybody else. They then devised a strategy. In order to ensure that everyone took part in the killing, they assigned each to kill specific Tutsis as they came along. This Christian refused to kill in spite of all the threats.

"Lord help me not to kill!" he prayed.

When his turn to kill came, he completely refused and they forced him to lie in a hole that had been dug. They were going to bury him alive. The militias took their shovels and began to cover him with soil.

"Give me some 5000 Frw and I will kill that man for you," one of the militias suddenly offered.

Out of fear, the Hutu Christian who was being buried alive then agreed to pay the militiaman the money. The militiaman went and killed the Tutsi who was standing a few meters away. The Hutu Christian was spared. But after the killing, the Hutu Christian became remorseful and refused to pay the militiaman the 5000 Frw he had offered him under compulsion.

"How can I pay you for shedding innocent blood?" the Hutu Christian asked.

Because of his refusal to pay, he was immediately killed also. This is one example of what happened to many Hutus whose conscience did not allow them to kill. Hutus who refused to kill were themselves killed without mercy.

An incident that is still vivid in my mind was that of Mr. Innocent. He was Tutsi and a well-known elementary school teacher. For both his kindness and the way he could transform unpromising pupils into high school raw material, all loved him. His class had a high pass rate in the whole *commune* where other schools could only have two students that would qualify for high school entry; his class always had the highest pass rate. Many parents transferred their children to this school where Mr. Innocent was the teacher.

Many killers would not touch Mr. Innocent and because of his goodness they tried to avoid killing him. Many were certain that even though he was Tutsi the militias would spare him.

But things were to change. One day a group of militias went to Mr. Innocent's house. Apparently he had just returned from the bush where he had gone to hide along with other Tutsis. Those involved in the killings knew him well. Controlled by the passion of the moment, one militiaman sunk a hoe in Mr. Innocent's head and he fell to his death. One among the group, possibly Mr. Innocent's former student, was disturbed at how callous and mindless the brutality had become.

"We have killed many, but the one who killed Mr. Innocent will never be forgiven by God!" he lamented.

Mr. Innocent's killer heard the remark and kept quiet. The militias reported back to their base and began to recount what they had accomplished. The one who had killed Mr. Innocent informed their leader that someone had condemned him for killing Mr. Innocent a Tutsi.

"What shall we do with the person who said that the killer of Mr. Innocent will not be forgiven by God?" the militiaman asked the leader in everybody's hearing.

"Is that person here?" asked the leader.

"Yes", the militiaman responded.

"Finish him!" the leader commanded.

Everybody converged on the boy who had made the sympathetic statement concerning the killing of Mr. Innocent. They knifed him to death. This act had a profound impact upon the group that seemed irretrievably sinking deeper into brutality. To make things worse, the twin brother of the one who had been killed was present. He wanted to run away for he could not stand the killing of his own brother. But he was afraid that this would only complicate things for him. He stood numbed by what he saw.

"What about his brother who is among us, do you think he will remain loyal to our group? Are we not creating enemies among ourselves?" someone asked.

"Also kill him!" the leader instructed.

The fate of his dead twin brother became his instantly. God seemed to stand at a distance, as Satan seemed to control the minds of people as they ruthlessly killed others.

No Place to Hide

7

Peace in Gitarama was short-lived. Rumors about killings were fast becoming reality. The father of my friend Jules realized that he had to hide us quickly lest his family become a target. Jules' father decided to take the five of us (Joel and Claudette, the brother and sister who had come from Ntongwe seeking refuge, Jules and his sister Jemime, and me) to Mr. Kalisa's home, one of his friends. We traveled a distance of 2 kilometers to Mr. Kalisa's home and upon arrival were told that the place was so infested with militias that it would be risky for us to stay at his home. We, however, managed to spend a night there but at dawn, Jules' father, unhappy with the security situation, took us back to his home.

When we arrived back at Jules' home his father asked us to remain behind as he went in search of possible refuge in the neighboring villages. We remained tucked under the beds for the whole day afraid that the militias would come at any moment.

At 2 .00 o'clock the following morning he came back with two Hutu boys, Eleazar and Janvier, who were to assist us to get to a place to hide. Because of our increasing numbers in this one home, it was becoming difficult to hide all of us in one place. Without wasting more time, we left together with the two boys for an unknown destination. Along the way they decided to go to Eleazar's home, one of the two boys that Jules' father had brought with him. We got to his home only to find it teeming with many other people who had come seeking for a place to hide. The home was small and could not take all of us. We could only remain there for one day.

Stories of looting, slaughtering of cows that belonged to Tutsis, and killings were floating everywhere. By the evening, rumors had spread around alerting the militias of our presence. We heard that they were planning to raid the village where we were. Some informed us that people were being mobilized to come and attack us in the night.

Up until this time in that area, if a Hutu man or woman were married to a Tutsi, the militias would not kill the spouse who was Tutsi. Eleazar, the Hutu boy in whose home we were hiding, suggested that the Tutsi girl, Claudette be regarded as his wife—the girl that had fled with her brother from South Ntongwe. None of us seemed opposed to his plan. We then left the girl at Eleazar's home and were again taken back to Jules' home. We knew that the reason we had left Jules' home in the first place was because it was no longer safe to remain there. But we found ourselves back where we had come from, since there seemed to be no other option.

Upon our arrival, we were reassured that the educated Hutus were not a target as had been rumored. This was good news for Jules and his sister. They did not need to worry any more. The problem now laid squarely on Joel, the boy whose sister had remained at Eleazar's home, and myself. We continued to panic because we expected the militias to come and kill us anytime. Jules' father like a sentinel, watched in every direction for any approaching danger. Inside the house Jules' mother fixed some food for us. We remained indoors and could only whisper for fear of detection. Our hearts continued to pound as we prayed for protection all night long.

Towards dawn, Jules' father entered the house in which we were hiding. He was troubled and posed a question.

"Where can I hide you?" he wondered in subdued tones.

He quickly remembered the sorghum plantation nearby. This was going to be a perfect place to send us. But as he continued to toy with the idea, he realized that the very fact that it seemed like a perfect hiding place would make it a target for the militias who were searching high and low for Tutsis. He then dismissed the idea of taking us to the plantation.

Joel, my young friend who accompanied me, became my traveling companion through all the difficulties of the genocide. He was young and nobody seemed to focus on him. Everybody we met addressed us as if I was the only one. In a sense the boy became my shadow. I remember there were times I would ask him to hide in a separate place so that if the militias found one of us at least the other would escape. He refused, opting to be with me wherever I went.

Finally, Jules' father came up with another idea. It was clear that he was in emotional pain and we knew that much as he cared for our safety, he was becoming increasingly worried for his own family's safety as well. We could tell the great agony that he felt as he announced the news to us.

"My sons its better you go to Ruhango *Underprefecture* (Sub-district)," he said. "There, instead of being killed by a machete, the soldiers will shoot you."

This was an option I reluctantly accepted. But when I considered that a fast death might be more endurable, I thought I would brave it and we would go as suggested. That same night, at around 3.00 o'clock in the morning we started for Ruhango *Underprefecture*, a distance of about 20 kilometers from Jules' home. Jules' father accompanied us halfway. He led the way and was walking so fast that we trotted behind him like chicks following a hen. He intended to take us halfway and be back home before sunrise. We penetrated thick forests and crossed several valleys trying to avoid any roadblocks along our way. The darkness before dawn only made our journey more difficult.

After climbing a few hills, Jules' father stood still and peering through the darkness of dawn pointed us to what appeared like a hill stretching ahead.

"Do you see those hills ahead?" he asked.

"Yes," I responded.

"You proceed. Ruhango *Underprefecture* is somewhere there!" he whispered.

Before he would let us go he held both of my shoulders with his hands and faced me.

"My son, I could feed you everyday of your life, but there is no place to hide you," he spoke with unmistakable emotion.

"You know that these people when they come to a home they search everywhere, including the ceiling. I do not know what to do for you," he continued.

"Go, perhaps you may be killed by a soldier's gun, that is better that a machete. If they kill you my son, I am sure that we will meet in heaven," he concluded his farewell words with tears in his voice.

He then prayed for us and gave me 4000 Frw before returning to his home leaving us to continue our formidable journey.

I greatly appreciated what Jules' father had done for us. He had already taken so many risks on our behalf and in addition out of his obviously limited resources had given me all that money. I was so grateful that in spite of my being Tutsi, he had embraced me as his own son. What love!

We trudged along groping in the darkness. It was difficult to see anything in the tall grass that engulfed us. We stumbled across fields and gardens suddenly coming to a line of houses. We retreated into the thick bushes for fear of being discovered. We were glad that there were no dogs to register our unintended arrival. As we plunged back into the bush, our confusion intensified. We were now lost with no sense of direction whatsoever. We seemed to go round in circles.

It was still dark when we found a path that we thought led to Ruhango *Underprefecture*. We had only walked less than 500 meters when we heard a group of people walking in our direction. They were plotting aloud, describing how they were going to kill someone within their village. We knew we were in harm's way so we squeezed through a wooden fence that ran along the left side of the road and hid in the thick bushes flat on our stomachs.

"He doesn't deserve to live!" one among the group shouted.

"Today is his last!" another echoed back.

"We must make sure his death is as painful as we can make it!" they seemed to build consensus as they walked past our hiding place.

We prayed and thanked God that He had spared us from these militiamen.

After they had gone past and we were certain that there were no more coming, we emerged but decided it was unsafe to continue on the road. We walked parallel to the road through the bush. We continued to stray into villages because of the tall grass and thick vegetation along our way. This was becoming risky because with the approaching day light people were beginning to wake up. We decided to go back to the main road.

No sooner had we come back to the road than we met a man carrying a machete, wearing shorts but no shirt. We thought that maybe he was following the other militiamen that we had seen earlier on. There was no way we could avoid him so we met head-on. I decided to whisper a prayer.

"Good morning" I greeted him.

"Good morning" he replied.

"May you show us the way to Ruhango *Underprefecture*?" I requested.

"Do you think you will pass through this place?" he asked.

"Give me your ID card!" he demanded.

I reached into my pocket and showed him my card, simultaneously praying that God would protect us once more.

"Are you Tutsi?" he asked.

"I'm neither Tutsi or Hutu," I answered.

"So you're Burundese," he inquired.

"No!" I replied.

"Why don't you give me money and I will let you pass through before others notice you?" he asked.

Since Jules' father had given me the 4000 Frw, I decided to carefully pull out part of that amount. I managed to fish out 1000 Frw and he accepted. He then showed us the way to Ruhango *Underprefecture* and we proceeded.

Hardly 500 meters down the road we approached what seemed to be a roadblock. There were many people standing as if waiting for something. They were not talking. Most of them had big towels wrapped around their heads and some were hanging around their necks. It seemed too late to run away so I decided to go right ahead and meet them. I began to pray again.

"Lord, don't forsake us!" I asked.

When we came to where the people were, I extended a hand of greeting. I reached out to all that I could shake hands with, but they seemed distant and confused. As I greeted them I asked, "Are you at a roadblock?"

None seemed eager to answer and it was difficult to tell whether it was due to mere reluctance or confusion.

"Bye, and have a good day!" I waved as we went past.

We left them standing dumbfounded, fully armed with their machetes and knives. God had intervened and performed another miracle.

It was much clearer now with the sun's rays warming our frozen fingers. I had thrown away my towel because I did not want anyone to think that we had slept in the bush or that we had traveled a long distance. We saw perched on a hill a church, and as we came closer we saw a sign that indicated that it was a Seventh-day Adventist church. I longed to go and rest at the church and possibly hide there too, but it was about two kilometers away. We decided to go nevertheless and we prayed for safe passage.

As we walked towards the church, we saw a group of women sitting beside the road. They looked tired and worn out and fear was written on their faces. There was something unusual about them. A certain woman was standing in front of the group and was addressing them. As we drew closer she stopped speaking and all eyes were on us. Although we initially were scared, our fear subsided when we discovered that they were equally afraid of us. They looked so desperate, confused, and frantic.

"Are you Tutsi?" the lady who had been addressing the group asked me.

"Yes!" I answered.

"Where are you going?" she asked.

"To Ruhango *Underprefecture*," I told her

She then warned us of how unsafe it was for us to go there and went into a detailed description of how people were being killed along the way.

"You will not reach your destination!" she stressed.

Her description of the horror ahead of us weakened me. I was so afraid that I wished she had not said anything. I preferred not knowing ahead of time. I was getting comfortable dealing with situations as they arose. I had become accustomed to emergencies in which I would call on God and He had always been ready to work out a miracle just in time. How was I to deal with this detailed foreknowledge?

"Go behind that house. Go behind that house!" she insisted repeatedly.

"The militias are coming!" she warned.

We rushed behind the house. Joel, my traveling companion, was still with me—the young man from Ntongwe. There was no decent place to hide for the house was on top of a mound and we could see across the valley a group of people busy slaughtering a cow. As we hid behind the house we heard a group of people talking loudly and others shouting mentioning the number and names of people who had not been killed. They discussed why it was important to urgently hunt down those still remaining and to kill them before it was too late. They went past and we seemed safe. I thanked God for another miracle.

After they were all gone the lady who had told us to hide behind the house came and asked us to follow her. We did not know where she was taking us. I knew she was Hutu. When we came to a house she asked us to come in and we did. She brought us some cassava. We ate and were very grateful for her hospitality although fear prevented us from fully enjoying the food. She asked us where we had come from. We told her that we had come from Kigali.

"My son, I wish I could hide you, but I don't know what to do!" she lamented.

"What church do you belong to?" she asked as she eyed the Bible in my hand.

"Seventh-day Adventist!" I said.

"That's my church also!" she cheerfully beamed.

She then offered prayer on our behalf. Before we could leave she spoke some words of encouragement.

"I am sure our God will be with you!" she assured us.

We thanked God for the words of hope that this lady had spoken. Once more, we were reminded that God had not abandoned us, and although faced with insurmountable odds, with God's help we would survive.

We left the woman's house and decided to go back to where we had come from—Jules' home. Yet as I thought of the roadblocks, my heart sunk. We thought that waiting for nightfall would be a good idea. So we decided to spend the rest of the day in hiding.

Where should we hide? This presented a dilemma. We scouted around but there was no thick vegetation to hide us. We made up our mind to go to the church that we had seen on the hill. On our way there we met a very old man. He asked us where we were going and we told him that we were going to church. He wondered why we would go to church when no one was at church because of the unrest. Nevertheless, he showed us the shortest road to the church and we set off, but when we came to a valley we decided to hide there since we found a nice spot. While in hiding, a militiaman dressed in banana leaves around his waist came to where we were. He looked so fierce.

"You must be Tutsi," he stated.

We were so afraid. We did not respond and he went by without asking further questions. God had done another miracle and our lives were spared once more.

Bargaining With The Killers

8

Around dusk we started back for Ntongwe, back to Jules' home. Going to Ruhango *Underprefecture* seemed more dangerous than retracing our steps. On this day people seemed busy feasting on the cows they had looted from their victims. Perhaps the festive mood deterred the militias from searching the bushes. After walking for one kilometer, someone saw us and came to us running. He was armed with a machete, and he asked for my ID card. I handed him the card.

"You're Tutsi!" he shouted.

"If you give me money, I will not kill you," he promised.

I quickly gave him 1000 Frw. As if that was not enough, he then violently cut the strap of my watch and took my watch. From a distance, other militias saw what he had done and they also realized that he was a stranger in their village.

"Don't give him the money," they protested. "You're ours!"

When the man saw the other militias approaching, he ran away with both my watch and the 1000 Frw.

The one that had been shouting from afar had now come to where I was. He had a bad odor about him of one who had not bathed in a long time. He was dirty with blood all over his clothes and when I saw his knife, chills went up my spine.

"Why did you give him the money?" he asked.

I was slightly relieved to see that his main focus, like the one before him, was money. If I gave him money, he might let me go, (I thought). I still had a bit of it remaining, so could bargain for my life and that of my companion.

"Give me money, or else I will kill you!" he demanded.

"Please don't kill me!" I pleaded trying to buy time.

"I can only help you if you give me some money!" he insisted.

"But don't give me 100 Frw!" he cautioned.

I thought to myself that since I had two 1000 Frw bills, I would pull out one of them. But before I could do so I told him that I could only afford to give him 300 Frw. This was way above what he had asked for.

He beamed a smile like a toddler that had received unexpected candy.

"You owe me 700 Frw!" I declared as I handed him the 1000 Frw bill.

He did not have change but promised to give it to me as soon a he found change. He then offered to escort us. Since he was familiar with the area and he knew exactly where the other militiamen were, he steered away from any possible danger. At some point he ordered us to remain while he went ahead of us. Apparently he knew that there was a roadblock and went to negotiate our safe passage since there was no option but to go through that place. He was gone for what seemed like eternity.

During his absence, two men came to where the militiamen had left us. They were also armed with machetes and we knew that we were in trouble. They drew close and leaned forward to see us more clearly under the moon lit sky.

"Don't be afraid!" I spoke out with a degree of feigned confidence.

Deceived by my courage, they assumed that I was Hutu and we began to chat. This was not deception for I had prayed to God for protection as I saw them approach. It was indisputable that God was with us. What we had experienced so far was beyond my wildest imagination. I had witnessed miracle upon miracle and I was left without any doubt of the miracles God is said to have performed and are written about in the Bible.

Our peace was short-lived. One of the two men studied my features and concluded that I was Tutsi, but he chose to keep it to himself. However, as our conversation continued, they asked us where we had come from. I told them that we had come from Kigali. Linking the fact that we had come from a place as distant as Kigali and given my Tutsi appearance, one of the men said, "You will be killed!" It was clear to us that these men were not enthusiastic militias but had been coerced into killing.

Our conversation was interrupted. The man who had gone to negotiate for our safe passage through the roadblock came running.

"No!" he shouted. "These people are mine!"

"If they are yours, give us money then we will hide them and they won't be killed!" one on the men responded.

Immediately a violent argument broke out between them. The two men demanded 150 Frw and the other man was only willing to offer them 100 Frw. But since he still owed me the 700 Frw in change, I urged him to give them the amount they were asking for so they would hide us. He was not keen.

After a long exchange of bitter words, the man with my 700 Frw turned to a nearby tree, raised his machete and struck one of its branches in anger.

"Do whatever you want!" he said. He then ran away, leaving us stuck with the two other militiamen.

"Please help us!" I begged.

"The only way to help you is if you give us money," they demanded.

Since I still had 1000 Frw remaining in my pocket, I bargained offering them 150 Frw. But since I did not have changed money, I gave him the 1000 Frw bill and asked him to give me change. He agreed to return my 850 Frw as soon as he would find change.

"Let's go!" one of the men motioned to us. "We will try to hide you!"

We traveled a short distance and came to a tiny grass-thatched hut. There was a fire on the heath and a woman carrying a baby on her back, was preparing some food. We shortly discovered that this woman was the wife of one of the two militiamen. She was told to take care of us as they went back on their patrol. We remained, praying all the time. The woman offered us some cassava bread with meat. But since I am vegetarian, I politely declined. The same God who had provided for all my needs would give us the appropriate food at the right time. I tried not to sound impolite, so I thanked the woman for her hospitality. She then gave us a mat on which to sleep. Before we could sleep, I prayed thanking God for all the protection he had given us.

We had hardly gone to sleep when the two men returned and woke us up.

"You have to leave right away!" one of the two men shouted impatiently. "People are coming to kill you!"

We jumped up and made our way to the door, but when we got outside, there were two additional men waiting for us.

"Who is this?" one of the new arrivals asked me as he came right up to my nose.

"They are my visitors!" the owner of the house replied.

"They are Tutsi!" he alleged.

They took the other two militiamen to task for having hidden us in their home. The men, who had brought us there now ordered us to leave for fear of their own safety, but seemed suspicious. I noticed that the one owing me the 850 Frw in change wanted us to leave without giving me change.

The new arrivals were now asking for money, but I did not have any more money except the 850 Frw still with the other militiamen. I begged them to share the 850 Frw among themselves. The owner of the house threw us out of his yard and the other two decided to take us to the nearest roadblock where they would kill us. On the way I continued to beg them to release us. They refused. I offered to return to the man with my 850 Frw so that I could get the money and give it to them. They agreed to this. We went back only to find that the man with my 850 Frw had disappeared.

Unwilling to release us, they led us back to the roadblock where the other militias were. My pockets were now empty and I could not use money any more to bargain. I turned to God in prayer. God was the only alternative since all the money had run out.

"Lord, you have been with me all the way. Why should I doubt your ability to protect me now? Our lives are at stake, please reveal yourself once again!" I entreated the Lord as I walked towards the roadblock.

It was around 3.00 o'clock in the morning. As we walked towards the roadblock we passed by a house. One of the two men escorting us told his colleague that he was going to quickly check whether everything was all right at his house since he had been away for some time. We continued walking. I thought this was the perfect opportunity to negotiate with the man who had remained with us.

"What value is my blood to you?" I posed the question to him.

"What do you benefit by killing me?" I rephrased it without giving him time to respond. "Why can't I give you my shoes and jacket and you let me go?"

He kept silent for some time. Then after a while, he said to me, "I will accept that!"

I stooped and loosed by shoelaces. I removed my shoes remaining only with my socks. I handed him the shoes and also my jacket. He grabbed them from me, wrapped my shoes in the jacket and hid them in a bush beside the path. Meanwhile, I removed my socks and slowly adjusted to life without shoes.

We proceeded with him and in the process of crossing a stream, a loud shout came from behind, but I couldn't understand what was being said. Instead of continuing with us, he decided to go back telling us that his life was also in danger. I wondered if he was returning out of fear for his own life, or was he returning out of fear that his ill-gotten parcel hidden in the bush would disappear.

After crossing the river we ran for a few meters and came upon a main road. The road was very stony making it difficult for me to run. My bare feet were now bleeding from the cuts so I decided to slow down and walk. I thought that it was better for us to leave the main road, as I was afraid we would meet more roadblocks. We decided to walk through the bush. Though it was still dark, I was regaining a sense of direction. I could tell the direction of Jules' village, the place where we intended to go. Stepping on thorns, bumping into stumps, sometimes falling in the mud, we went down into a valley, and painful as it was continued to move. After traveling for some time we decided to rest briefly. I was all dirty with blood coursing down my legs and feet. I was in great pain.

As I sat debating with my companion whether to continue, we saw two men coming in our direction. When they saw us they stopped, but it was too late to escape. They were supporting themselves with walking sticks and this was a relief to us since they were not wielding the infamous machetes. We could tell they were shaken thinking that we might be militias.

"Do not be afraid!" I assured them. "Where are you going?"

"Ruhango," they replied.

They explained that they were going to Ruhango to hide. I told them not to go since I had heard of brutal killings there. I also told them not to go to the village where we had recently come from because they had robbed me of all my money and that it was due to divine miracles that we had escaped. As I was busy sharing what we had gone through, one of the two men could not remain standing any more. His knees gave in.

"We are coming from Ntongwe *Commune* and 7000 people have been killed. We thought we had escaped, it's the same wherever we go!" he sobbed uncontrollably.

These two men had escaped from Ntongwe *Commune*. We learned that in Ntongwe, Government soldiers had gathered Tutsis supposedly offering them protection. The militias and refugees from Burundi were then ordered to surround the Tutsis and kill all those who tried to escape as the soldiers gunned them down. This was the situation from which the two men we met had fled.

I was touched by the despair of the two men. My heart went out to them, particularly to the man that was sobbing.

"Stand up, I am going to pray for you," I said and reached out to lift the man who was sitting down. I laid my hands on their shoulders as I prayed for them.

"Lord, you have protected these men from Ntongwe to this place. I am sure you are still capable of taking care of them. You know and see everything that is happening. I ask you Lord that their lives may have value in your sight and even if they may die, please enable us one day to meet in your kingdom. Amen."

After the prayer, both men became remarkably strong.

"I now understand why God led me to you!" the man who had been sobbing a few minutes ago declared.

"I'm no longer afraid," he confided.

"Be strong. God is going to be with you," I said.

We bade them farewell as we got up to leave but they decided they wanted to follow us. I dissuaded them saying, "Trust in God. He will be with you. I am as vulnerable as you."

They stayed behind and I never saw them again.

I was more and more confident of where we were to go. We arrived at Mr. Kalisa's home—the place we had been hidden once before. We found Mr. Kalisa at home after three days of our absence. He asked where we had come from. After we told him, he was afraid and pleaded with us to leave. He told us that the militias were coming to his home as frequently as three times a day to search and see whether he was not hiding any Tutsis. Mr. Kalisa was a Hutu Seventh-day Adventist and the militias specifically targeted their searches on Christians like him. Understanding our dilemma, he later decided to hide us. He took us to his cassava plantation. There was a heavy rain and fog reduced visibility almost to zero. I was, however, worried that my white shirt would make me easy to detect. I dipped it in mud hoping that the dirt would camouflage me as I tried to hide. Unfortunately my efforts to tint my shirt proved futile—it was not dark enough!

That morning around 10 o'clock, a group of people numbering about twenty came and combed Mr. Kalisa's cassava plantation, hand in hand like one big net, to make sure they made a thorough search. As they approached where we were hiding they shouted repeatedly: "Power, Power, Power!" This was the slogan for all the parties that had joined the killing. This slogan had become a way the militias greeted each other. It was therefore a sign of their absolute control of any area where they were killing people.

Upon hearing the shout, "Power!" I prayed for protection. Now they were less than ten meters from where we were hiding. Then something unusual happened.

"Power, Power, Power!" one militiaman close to where I was hiding shouted.

Then every one of them echoed the shout as they ran in the opposite direction. I did not know what had happened but Mr. Kalisa did. He saw it from his pineapple garden where he was working. The militias had discovered someone hiding right next to where we were and they abandoned the search and began to chase after that person whom they later killed about a kilometer from where we were. We were glad to have been spared but at the same time saddened by the loss of someone's life in our place.

Digging My Own Grave

9

We continued hiding in Mr. Kalisa's cassava plantation until we were sure that the group of militias, that had stampeded after the man they had discovered close to where we were hiding, were all gone. Suspicious that upon their return the militias may wish to start where they had stopped their search, we shifted to another hiding place. It was just a stone's throw from the cassava field, in a patch of reeds mixed with some tall grass and bushes. We crawled slowly and carefully making sure that the grass on our path remained as unruffled as possible.

When it began to rain again we saw this as a mixed blessing. If we decided to change our hiding place we could move a little faster because the wind and the rain swayed the grass violently and our movements would not be as conspicuous. But the bad part was that the rain soaked our clothes and we felt very cold. Earlier, I had helped Joel to hide separately about ten meters from my own hiding place. When he could not endure tormenting ants and torrential down pours of rain, he decided to join me. He came to where I was and told me that he would rather die with me huddling for warmth, than freeze in isolation. We remained in hiding until evening. The militias did not come back and we thanked God for this.

After dark, we decided to leave Mr. Kalisa's place for Jules' home. This proved to be a difficult journey. It took us more than four hours to cover a distance of about 2 kilometers. We tried to be as careful as we could, making sure that our feet would not make any noise as we stepped on dry leaves and branches through the thickets. We would pause now and then to survey every bush or tree to make sure it was not a figure of some militiaman waiting to kill.

Eventually, we arrived at Jules' home. It must have been around 2.00 o'clock in the morning. I knocked at the door. Jules' mother, then in her sixties, came to open the door. As soon as she recognized me, she broke down into tears.

"Where are you coming from?" she inquired.

As I began to recount all that we had gone through, Jule's father came and listened to our story. They were glad that we were still alive, yet sad that we had come back because the militias were conducting ruthless searches and they feared that all of us, including them, were going to be killed. What complicated matters was that during my previous stay at this home, I had gone to church and preached and word had gone around that Jules had brought a Tutsi preacher from Kigali. Because of this militias had molested Jules' family accusing them of hiding me. Unconvinced, the militias would come at awkward times repeatedly to search for me. So my returning was only going to worsen things for them.

"My son, you're going to be killed!" Jules' mother told me as she sobbed.

"I hate to see them spill your blood," she continued.

"Why cry?" I asked as if unaware of what was at stake. "I will not die. God will protect me!" I protested.

"That's childish!" she replied. "Even Christians are being killed."

She then counted and named the Christians that had since been killed within their village.

"I don't worship another person's God. My God, the one who protected me in Kigali until now will protect me!" I spoke with conviction.

Realizing my conviction in God's protection, she became quiet. Meanwhile Jules' father stood lost in thought. Then he broke his silence.

"Where am I going to hide you?"

He seemed stranded. He had already sent one of his sons to check around his home to make sure that none of the militias were coming. After toying with so many options, he thought of one bush area in Gasuna village, about two or so kilometers from Jules' home.

"Let's try it," he said. "I believe that your God will protect you!"

At about 3.00 o'clock in the morning we started off for Gasuna village. Jules' father led the way. We walked through thickets, ravines, and a swollen river. We felt tired, but we continued until we came to the bush area he had in mind. We penetrated the heart of the bush and knelt as he prayed for our safety. After this, he returned to his home. We remained in the bush.

Hiding in this bush, I had time to pray to God and also to reflect on the kindness of Jules' father. He had done all he could and I was so thankful for all the help that he had given us. He had risked so much for us. When we left his home he had wanted to give me his only coat to make me warm since it was very cold. One thing, however, prevented him; since people in his village knew them well including the items of clothing they wore, if I was found wearing his coat they would know that he had given it to me. That would get him into serious trouble with the militias. Instead, he gave us some old and dirty sacks to keep us warm—the dirt was immaterial, what mattered was warmth. It rained all night and the sacks became drenched.

It was now about ten or eleven o'clock in the morning when we heard a shout followed by a conversation from people who were approaching our hideout.

"People might be hiding here," someone intimated.

"Even if we may not kill them, the snakes will," another man answered.

Then a dog came where I was hiding and began to whine. I peeped through the corner of the sack covering my head. The dog would not move. It continued to make a strange noise while staring at me. I tried to scare it away but that only made it whine louder.

"You had better surrender!" one man commanded me as he beckoned his friends who were already a few meters past where we were hiding.

"It's two of them. I have found them!" he celebrated.

"Come out!" they commanded.

I stood up, holding the plastic bag that contained my Bible and all my earthly possessions. I made my way towards the militias who impatiently waited for me. My companion followed. I extended my hand to shake the first man's hand but he refused. I tried to greet the second man; this one accepted and shook my hand. Another man came to me and asked for my ID card. I gave it to him. Just as he was studying my ID we heard a loud bang. Apparently someone had been shot hardly a hundred meters or so away.

"We are going to kill you," the man holding my ID card told me.

They then sandwiched us taking us to the place where they were going to kill me. I was afraid to die. I observed that most of these militias did not have machetes but knives and nail-studded clubs called "Ntampongano" which means, "there is no bribe you can pay to redeem yourself." I therefore begged them to shoot me, rather than stab me.

"No!" one of them protested.

We came to a certain village where some people were already gathered. After a quick survey of the landscape near one of the houses, a suitable spot was selected. This is where I was to dig my grave.

"We don't have bullets to waste," one militiaman shouted.

"Take that hoe and dig your own grave. We don't want to strain ourselves. Dig the grave then we will kill you and bury you there!" another militiaman shouted as the rest of them echoed in agreement.

I was tired but since I had no option I took the hoe and began digging my own grave. My companion, Joel stood watching as I dug the grave. As I started to dig, I also started to pray and confidently hoped that before the digging was over, God would intervene.

"Lord, I know you will save me because I know you are with me. Send your angel to protect me," I pleaded with God in prayer.

"Do something, Lord! Whatever you choose, that will be fine with me, if you send fire to burn or scatter them that will be alright, if you send thunder and lightening, still that is alright." I continued to pray as I dug.

As I continued digging, one of the militias took my Bible where I had laid it. He combed it from cover to cover, it seems. I noticed that he was becoming curious about the highlighted sections throughout the Bible.

"What do these colors mean?" he asked. "And why are they different?"

"The underlined verses strengthen me spiritually. I use them for preaching," I responded taking advantage of a short break from my digging.

The man continued to leaf through the Bible, his interest deepening. He seemed to have gone beyond a mere admiration of the various colors I had used. He seemed to reflect on what he was reading.

"Keep digging," one man ordered. "Don't waste our time. We have other things to do."

I resumed digging.

"Brother!" the militiaman that had been reading my Bible called and then paused with sincerity written on his face.

"Brother?" Did I hear right? What was I to make of this? Was it just a slip of the tongue or what? Was God beginning to answer my long-overdue prayer for deliverance?

"Before you die, I beg you to give me this Bible so I may read it," he continued to speak, raising my hope for a miraculous rescue.

"That should be fine," I replied. "You may have it."

"That Bible does not belong to you alone. It also belongs to us!" one militiaman standing towards the back of the crowd objected. "If you want it, give us some money!" he demanded.

"Whatever amount you may ask, I will give you!" the man holding my Bible replied.

This seemed a fair compromise because calm suddenly returned to a crowd that had erupted into commotion.

I continued digging. I was still praying, but now with a degree of impatience because God seemed to take His time. Didn't He see that I was almost done digging? Didn't He realize that I was about to be killed?

Moved more by impatience than pity, one of the militias stepped into the pit and pushed me aside.

"This man will delay us!" he said.

As the man dug the grave, I continued to pray for God to intervene.

Then suddenly, one of the militias shouted, "No, brothers!" "That's not fair!" he complained.

Everybody wondered what had happened. The man laid out his arguments.

"Why should we bury this stranger in our field? We don't know this man. Why not let him go and dig a new grave away from our field somewhere by the road? This piece of land on which you wish to bury this man is private property. This stranger should not be buried on our land. Instead, we should let him dig another grave along the main road for that is State property. We should use this ready grave to bury our friend's brother-in-law!" he spoke with conviction.

Everybody nodded unanimously to the suggestion.

As I later learned, this dead man was the one shot right at the time we had been discovered while hiding in the bush a few minutes earlier. He was Tutsi but his sister was married to one of the Hutus. In order to make death easier for him they had decided to shoot him instead of slicing him by machete.

They brought the body of the man and after they had laid him in the grave, one man offered a short prayer.

"Mary, Mother of Jesus, receive him!" he prayed.

After the prayer that had been offered, several men repeated prayers that were incoherent. Initially, I was upset by their mockery of God but later realized that they were possibly acting out of ignorance.

Then some heavily built men took shovels and began to cover the grave with soil. They took turns and in no time the burial was over.

Immediately, something happened to me. I felt a strange kind of courage creep over me and I prayed. I forgot my own plight and focused on theirs.

"Lord, these people don't know you. Help me now. Even if I may die, allow me to say something that will change their lives for the better. Don't let me die before I tell them who you are!" I prayed.

After burying the other man, they led me to the new gravesite. As we approached the place, one of the leaders made an announcement.

"Please don't help him dig the grave this time. He must dig it himself and we will bury him alive!" he said.

"We are going to kill you but..." another man spoke but did not complete his sentence.

Before digging, I mastered some courage and asked: "But why do you want to kill me?"

"Are you not Tutsi?" one of them replied.

"I'm Christian!" I replied.

"But even if you're not Tutsi, the children that you will bear will be Tutsi, they will be our enemies!" he argued.

When Killers Wept

The second gravesite was very close to the road, beyond any privately owned property. It made much sense for the militias to bury me beside the road because that land belonged to the Government. As I surveyed the site I realized that it provided a beautiful setting for preaching. There was short green grass as well as smooth stones on which the people could sit and listen to my last sermon.

"May you please give me my Bible so I may say something before digging my grave?" I asked the man who was holding my Bible.

"No!" one man protested. "What are you going to teach us? We don't want you to teach us anything! What can a Tutsi teach us anyway? You are our enemy!"

"What can he teach us," another man contested.

The militiamen were divided. Some were willing to let me speak while others were totally opposed to the idea. After some intense debate, one man proposed a solution.

"Anyone who does not care to listen to him should close their ears and let those who wish to listen go ahead. After all we don't know what he has to say. We don't know what he will say. After his speech we will kill him." He argued.

"While we have a right to kill him, we don't have the right to deny him to speak before he dies," the man who had been studying my Bible argued as he handed me my Bible.

I did not totally agree with his logic because I did not believe that anyone had a right to kill anybody. I, however, was grateful to God for prompting this man to convince his fellow militias to let me to say something before I died.

"Go ahead and speak your last words," the leader of the crowd commanded.

I looked for a strategic position—a place where everyone could not only hear my voice but also see me. Anticipation swelled as my eyes scanned the crowd. I was ready to speak. I cannot take credit for what happened at that moment. I believe that God simply took over. I was filled with power and authority. I began by expressing my gratitude.

"Thank you for your kindness in allowing me to say something before you kill me," I said this from the bottom of my heart.

I was grateful to my captors because I knew of instances where people were not given any permission to say anything before their death. I recalled how some Christians had been derided by their captors who alleged that God was dead that's why He could not come to their rescue.

"I wish to commend you for praying before burying your dead as you did a few minutes ago," I paused. "But there is something you need to know."

I noticed that the minute I began to speak the crowd increased in number. It was no longer the militias alone, but also villagers returning from their fields, and also people traveling along the road came to listen. I noticed children, mothers, and many elderly people compete to catch a glimpse of what was happening. After I had been discovered in the bush, word had quickly spread that I was a Tutsi soldier and a commander and that the militias were going to torture me until I disclosed where I had hid the guns. So many came driven by curiosity to see this stranger experience a brutal death.

"It's better to let people pray for themselves before they die because, after they are dead, your prayers have no value whatsoever," I continued.

I opened my Bible and turned to Ecclessiates 9:5 and read, "The living know that they will die, but the dead know nothing. They have no further reward even the memory of them is forgotten. Their love, hate, jealousy have long since vanished. Never again will they have a part in anything that happens under the sun."

"You should not ask anyone to pray for you after you die. Now, while you are still alive, is the time to pray for yourself. This is the chance you have to place your life in God's hands," I declared.

"I am not asking for your pardon, because I know that you will only do what God will allow you to do, but I want you to understand what is going on now. You're fighting a war whose nature you know nothing about," I spoke uninterrupted.

"This war is not about Hutus against Tutsis or Tutsi against Hutus because there are many Tutsis and Hutus who are not part of this. This war is between Jesus Christ and Satan," I explained.

"As you know, many innocent people are being killed. The issue is not this current death, for everyone will eventually die. But the real issue is the eternal death for it is final. Those who obey God don't need to fear this present death because when Jesus comes they will live again. But those that disobey God will perish forever. The second death is the death that all of us should fear. Many Hutus and Tutsis refuse to be involved in this ongoing conflict because they know the truth."

I turned my Bible to 1 Peter 2:9, and then read: "But you are a chosen people a royal priesthood, a holy nation, a people belonging to God that you may declare the praise of him who called you out of darkness into this wonderful light."

As I began to comment on this verse, I could see streams of tears flowing down several cheeks. Many desperately tried to conceal their tears, so they went behind some bushes in order to wipe their eyes. I continued unabated as if oblivious to their tears.

"In this conflict, the chosen ones are from all tribes. These no longer place their ethnic identity before their new identity of being chosen by God. The chosen ones practice love, unity, and peace. But Satan who is on the other side of the struggle wants to destroy all of God's people. But even if God's chosen people may die, they die in Christ and He will give them eternal life. Satan is cruel he wants to destroy those that have not chosen God. He wants them to die without knowing about God's love. He tells them about their tribal differences and purported superiority. He incites them to hate and kill those that are not of their tribe. As a result, many are working for Satan without knowing." I continued to preach.

"I'm not asking you to release me because I know that soon these wars of the world will end. And if the Lord wants me to rest now, I am willing to sleep until He comes to resurrect His people," I paused.

As I was concluding my speech, I could see lots of commotion. The militias and other observers were forming groups of threes and fours, consulting, and at times arguing. I didn't know exactly what was going on, but there was so much agitation and weeping. It seems like God had spoken to their hearts as confirmed by their tears. I believed that God had given them a chance to make up their mind. They could now decide on whose side to stand in the ongoing conflict.

"I can now dig my grave, then I will say my last word before you kill and bury me," I announced.

When he realized that I was concluding my sermon that must have lasted for about twenty minutes, a certain man who had stressed how brutal they were going to kill me, sprang from where he was sitting.

"I know that I had instigated that we kill this man mercilessly," he confessed.

"But if any of you decide to kill this man, may his blood be on you, not me!" he shouted waving his pointed finger to the crowd.

In hearing this, everybody went wild. They cried out, "Let him go! Let him go! Let him go!"

The leader of the militias stepped forward and asked all the spectators: "Do you agree that we should let him go?"

"Yes!" they shouted in one voice.

"We will let you go," he said. "But before we do so, let me caution the women among us. Since you are notorious for gossiping. If any of you leaks the information that we released this "Inkotanyi" (Rwanda Patriotic Front soldier), we will be killed. But before we get killed, we will kill whoever releases this information," the leader spoke with great authority.

"If you decide to release me, please allow me to pray for you," I said.

"Please pray for us," they responded in a chorus.

The situation had changed. Hearts seemed to have been softened. God had spoken to his children and they were no longer the same. They didn't seem to know what to do with their machetes, knives and the rest of their instruments of torture. I closed my eyes and began to pray.

"Lord, you showed yourself to your people today. Thank you for choosing men and women, boys and girls from all tribes of the world. What is happening now is not concealed from your eyes—you see it all. Thank you for making your children hear and accept your word, which is the truth, we all need. You know these children of yours very well. Forgive them. Thank you for speaking through me. I know Satan is angry and wants all to perish. Please don't allow him. Now Lord, may your grace shine upon them and have mercy on them. Amen."

The leader selected two heavily built young man to escort me and my companion to a place where we could hide for fear that other groups of militias might harm us. The two escorts picked up their nail-studded clubs and we followed them leaving the crowd behind us.

Caring Killers 11

We traveled for a distance of about five kilometers and came to a small grass-thatched hut. This was the home of one of the two young men who had accompanied us. We had to bend much in order to go in. They gave us some wooden stools on which to sit. After a few minutes they fixed some cassava bread with some meat for us to eat. I ate the cassava bread instead because I did not want the hardships of the war to divert me from my vegetarianism. I had purposed to remain firm in my dietary habits and other areas of my life.

At moments like these, I had often drawn much inspiration and encouragement from Christian authors and one of these is Ellen G. White who notes in her book entitled: *Education* that:

> The greatest want of the world is the want of
> men—men who will not be bought or sold, men
> who in their inmost souls are true and honest, men
> who do not fear to call sin by its right name, men
> whose conscience is as true to duty as the needle is
> to the pole, men who will stand for the right
> though the heavens fall.[1]

When I politely refused to eat the meat they had offered me, our hosts became curious.

"So Seventh-day Adventist don't eat meat?" one of
them asked.

"Some eat but others don't. I have decided not to eat,"
I responded.

We continued with our conversation and they seemed
satisfied with the explanation I had given them. After the
meal we slept and there were no disturbances during the
night.

The two young men were very kind to us. They went
to great lengths to find beans so they could give me vegetarian meals. They also brought out many ripe bananas
that had been buried behind the small hut. From their
regular patrols, they brought back lots of meat from cows
that had once belonged to Tutsis.

A new problem soon arose as we continued to stay in
the small hut. There was an elderly lady, a grandmother to
one of the young men, who lived with the young man in

this home. She was insane, maybe because of her old age. Often she would break into tears and cry out loud. At other times she would talk loudly wandering around the hut.

"Who are these people that I see here?" she would ask. "Where do they come from and what do they want in my home?"

I feared that she would call people's attention to our presence in this home and we would be killed. The grandmother was so incoherent and loud that we felt we should leave.

Just as we were contemplating this, a message was sent to the two young men who were taking care of us not to let us leave since there was so much killing going on in the surrounding area. They feared we would be in great danger so we complied and stayed. We postponed our departure indefinitely.

Although it had been stressed that ladies should not leak any information concerning our release after the preaching incident, rumors of what had happened quickly spread. Upon their return from a routine patrol, the two young men informed us with much sadness that we were now in danger because news of our whereabouts had spread. One of the young men had earlier assured us that soon the war would end and that none would kill us since he could hide us in a secret hole close to his home. But now things had changed. The young men were so different. We could tell they also feared for their lives.

"Go out!" the young man in whose home we were hiding demanded. "They are going to kill us!" "The whole village already knows that you are here. They will definitely kill all of us, so go out!"

I begged him to let us stay a little longer until dark. He refused.

"You go, your God will protect you," he spoke with confidence. "But as for me, I know they are coming to kill me for I have protected you." I appreciated their predicament and I felt sorry for them.

We had no choice but to leave. Around 11.00 o'clock in the morning we crawled and at times moved on our tummies in the bean field making sure we remained as invisible and undetectable as possible. We hid ourselves a stones-throw from the hut. We lay on our backs since lying on our sides would have made us visible above the short bean plants. We spent the whole day laying on our backs and all the time praying for God's protection.

We could hear lots of people passing by, since we were close to the road. We praised God that they were not able to see us. From the conversation of those who walked past, we could hear very clearly how the genocide was progressing. Some were celebrating their successes, while others were aspiring to do more: to find and to kill all the Tutsis who had not yet been discovered.

---

[1] Ellen G. White, Education, Mountain View, CA: Pacific Press Publishing Association, 1952, p. 57.

Ready to Die For a Tutsi

12

A fter hiding in the bean garden the whole day until nightfall, Joel, my companion, and I decided that we should go back to the bush close to Jules' home. There seemed to be no other place we could go to. On the following day we waited until evening and then went back to Jules' home. That same night Jules and his brother, Karara accompanied us back to the same bush we had come from. This bush was to become our home for the next 21 days that followed.

It was Saturday evening. I had spent the whole day reading my Bible, mostly the letters of Paul. For some reason I thought of starting from the book of Acts. In between Bible study, I prayed for strength to undertake the difficult task that lie ahead. I was determined to emerge from my hiding, and go and preach to the militias once more. I wondered if this was possible? My fear was that some of them had become so hardened that to preach to them would be a waste of time. I also feared for my life. My fear increased as I remembered my friend Jules' insistence at our last meeting that there was no reason for taking chances with my life in such a venture. Jules had reiterated the folly of hoping to convert a handful of militias in a country teeming with countless people bent on killing. What difference would that make? There was obviously no way anyone could convince all militias to listen to what I had to say.

In spite of such doubts, I was convinced that preaching to the militias was dependent on the power of the Holy Spirit and not my own power. I reminded myself that my life was not dependent on how the militias would react to the message I had to preach. God could use me the same way He had done in the past. I was going to tell them about God's love and then leave my safety in God's hands. Beyond anything else, my desire was to die victoriously—victorious in this case meant that I would courageously tell them of God's love and call them to repentance. I was sick and tired of living in the bush. I could not bear it anymore.

Why should I continue to languish in the bush if God was really on my side? With each passing moment, my desire to leave bush life increased. I was also tired of going to people's homes seeking refuge. During that Saturday, as I was reading the book of Acts, I was inspired by Paul's sufferings. I read the story about the hardships that Paul faced. In spite of his sufferings, Paul continued to preach from city to city. What a heroic life!

My mind raced through the Bible to other Bible characters that had endured suffering for God's sake. Names like Jeremiah, Elijah, Job, and many others came to mind. As I contemplated their sterling examples, my courage swelled. I was encouraged and felt that I too could live a life fully devoted to the honor and glory of God.

Immediately, I began to praise God as I asked for forgiveness. How could I ever get so discouraged? I poured out my heart in prayer saying, "Lord, you know the reason why I'm here in this bush. I now know that you have a purpose for me. Let me not consider my suffering anymore. Please strengthen my aching body and help me to be patient until you decide what you would have me do. Help me to see beyond my current situation and make me like clay in the hand of the potter. After my sufferings, allow me to go out and do what you want me to do for you."

My prayer was marked with desire for repentance for my sins. I remembered all the minute details of my whole life. Unkind words that I might have spoken, duties I had neglected, tasks I had not accomplished, all these came into full focus as I reviewed my past. I recalled how the Lord had miraculously protected me from Kigali to Gitarama. I remembered April 9 when the militias had come to my house while still in Kigali. I recalled how my helper had informed me that these men were our neighbors. I regretted that I had never told them about the love of Jesus Christ before the war broke out. Perhaps if I had done my part as a Christian they might have not become killers. I asked the Lord to forgive me of my sins of omission and I promised God that I was prepared to leave the bush and begin to speak for Him wherever He would send me.

That Saturday night when Jules came, I was a changed man. I felt so peaceful in spite of increasing physical suffering. When I saw him I was eager to share my experience with him. I had made a discovery. Not only had I discovered who the Lord was, but also who I was. My inner struggle had ended when I surrendered my will and life to God. I felt forgiven and ready to start a new life beaming with confidence.

Unfortunately, when Jules came that evening he looked very downhearted. I knew something was terribly wrong. Having known Jules for years, I could only guess that he had some bad news to tell me. After much persuasion, he told me that things were getting worse.

"You cannot hide in this bush anymore," he confided.

"Why? What has happened?" I inquired.

Jules began to tell me of the recent meeting that the militias had held. It had been decided that in order to make sure that nobody could hide anymore, everybody in the village was supposed to search every neighboring bush and keep their own fields free of any Tutsi who may wish to hide. If a Tutsi were found hiding in anyone's garden, that person together with his whole family would be killed.

Jules told me of how his mother could not sleep for fear that the killers would one day discover that I was hiding in the bush close to their house and that they would come kill all her children, her husband and her self. She had attempted to convince her husband, to tell me to leave the bush. After much discussion, Jules parents tried to make him understand that it made no sense to risk the life of their entire family for an individual who would eventually be killed.

As he unveiled my fate, I fought resentment by objectively appreciating the things Jules and his family had done for me so far. They had gone through a lot for me. They really didn't have to. They had tried their best to protect me, to hide me from house to house, and from bush to bush. Jules' parents had given me food, and were daily risking the life of their son, who every night braved the rain and real possibility of meeting the killers, to bring me and Joel, my young companion, food in our hiding place.

I further reasoned that I should not ask for anything beyond what is humanly possible. Why would a parent do something to endanger his children? Many people died at the hands of neighbors that had turned brutal and I decided that there was no need for my friend Jules' family to be killed just because of me.

The fact that the few days in our hiding place had been relatively safe did not mean that the war was over. It was clear to me that no one had any solution to our plight. Only God could solve this problem for us.

After this discussion with Jules, I began to understand why he was so worried. It was obvious that there was no other bush we could hide in. His parents had given him a week to find another bush in which to hide Joel and me. Jules was in a dilemma. Would he prize our friendship above the life of his own family? Was he now going to bid us farewell? When he told me that there was no other bush in which we could hide and he explained to me what had happened. I froze in silence. I had nothing to say.

Leaving this bush, which had become our home meant facing the militias. To complicate things, my body was aching and I felt sickly. I could hardly walk. What then were we going to do? I remembered all past miracles of how God had helped me preach to the militias. Even if I were to go and meet the militias, how would I preach to them? My throat was lined with painful sores making me unable to talk. I wondered if Jules was finally discouraged? Was he now prepared to let us go our way and die? Although I longed to continue relying on his protection and acts of mercy (bringing me food), I felt it was unfair for me to expect him to be alienated from his family be-cause of me and Joel.

"Jules, I know you have done all you can to help me," I said. "What do you make of my situation? Is this our last moment together?"

I realized that I was giving a mixed message to Jules. On the one hand I was clearly appreciative of all his sacri-fices for me. But when I asked for his opinion on what he thought of my predicament and also asked whether this was to be our last time together, I might have cornered him. But knowing the depth of our friendship, I felt free to share everything with him, including my own confu-sion over what was to happen to me.

"Your death will be mine and wherever you go, I will go too," he spoke with tears gushing from his eyes. "I will be with you till death and if we should survive I will be with you."

You cannot imagine the peace that flooded my heart at hearing such words from such a committed friend. There was still somebody in this world to share my sorrow! I was cheered to know that in Jules I had a true friend, one who was even ready to die for me. I felt very much strengthened.

"There is a God in heaven that cares about us, who knows the beginning from the end," I pointed out. "He loves us and nothing can happen to me with out his per-mission. Let's tell him about it and give him the week they have given us for a deadline to leave this place, so that He may answer our prayer. Since none of us can find an alternative hiding place or a solution to this problem we should trust in Him who is able to help us."

I then asked Jules to fast for a week, from that Saturday until the following Saturday. We prayed together and he went back to his home.

During the week that followed, hardly a minute would pass without me either praying or reading some portion of scripture. I thanked the Lord for His willingness to listen to my prayers. Every verse I read seemed to generate another positive perspective to my situation. My confidence in God was unassailable.

I expressed to God how thankful I was that He had shown me His hand all the way from Kigali until now. I praised God for having protected me in the bush where I now was. I remember telling God that I did not understand why He loved me the way He did. I prayed: "You know that I can no longer stay in this bush. Lord, you know that I don't have any other place to go. Nobody can receive me in his or her home without getting into danger. I'm now like a hunted animal. The only place I can go to is to you. I have no house or home. Look! Lord, even the bush you had given me during my suffering is being taken away and I have to leave in one week's time. Lord, I come to you, please provide an answer to my problem. This one week that they have given me, I also give it to you so that you may do another miracle. At the end of this week, show them that I am your servant and that you are my God. You know Lord, that I have faith in you, but if it is weak in your sight, Lord I ask that you may increase it so that my prayers will be acceptable to you."

During that entire week I prayed bargaining with God, reminding Him of the time I used to preach every Wednesday before the genocide broke out. I pointed God's attention to the many evangelistic efforts that I had conducted. I said: "Lord, you know I have trusted in you. I believe that your promises are all true and I am convinced that if we pray in faith you always answer. Now it is time for you to intervene and prove your love for me. Show them that you are a God who doesn't change."

Although I was asking my God to perform a miracle, I also asked Him not to let me leave without a chance to thank the family that had hidden me for all this time. I thought it appropriate to remind Jules' mother to continue trusting in God even when things seemed hopeless. I wanted to affirm that God is always in control in all the affairs of the world and that He does whatever is necessary to protect His people until the end.

In the bush, day after day and night after night, I had lost count of what day of the week it was. It is not surprising that when Thursday evening arrived, I thought it was already Friday. I was waiting for the end of the week with great anticipation because Saturday evening was the deadline I had given God to take me out of the bush. I knelt and worshipped the Lord confident that this was going to be the second last evening I was to spend in the bush before God would deliver me. Although I did not know exactly how God would do it I trusted that He was going to do something remarkable. I believed the Lord had already accepted my weeklong prayers.

I decided to stop asking God for anything, instead I began to pour out my heart thanking Him in advance for the anticipated deliverance. The following day, I was convinced that it was Saturday, the end of the critical week of fasting. The day came and passed but nothing happened. What I only heard was some shooting not far from where we were. This was of course in contrast to the distant shooting I had heard previously. What puzzled me, however, was the mixture of the sounds from the guns and the noise from the heavy thunder since it was raining.

While the shooting was going on, a thought crossed my mind. I thought that perhaps it was the "Inkotanyi" or Rwanda Patriotic Front Army approaching. I reasoned that this could be God's way of rescuing me. But this prospect presented some real problems. What would I do if they asked me to join them and fight? I reminded myself of an earlier decision that I had made. I was not going to kill anyone. I was going to live for God by telling the world that the Lord was coming soon. As soon as I asserted my identity and mission in life, I dismissed the thought of hoping to be delivered by an army, for that would bring me a lot of complications.

I kept expecting another way of deliverance but there was nothing in sight. I continued to battle mosquitoes, as had been the routine for days. I was very exhausted. Somehow when evening came, I felt a surge of strength. My hope soared as I pinned my faith on the fact that something grand was going to happen before sunset. I was totally disappointed and confused when the sunset came and night approached. I tried to be optimistic. I decided to pray and wait for my friend Jules who was going to come to me at the end of our week of fasting.

Jules finally came that evening. I quickly asked him about any news.

"Has God answered our prayers?" I asked.

"Not yet," he responded. "But let us keep on praying."

He did not have any news; instead he motioned that we should fall on our knees to pray. I was very discouraged. For a moment, I lost faith in prayer and didn't feel like praying. I was angry with God. I had prayed and asked God to show Himself either through Jules or anyone else but He seemed to have chosen to remain silent. Was there anything wrong in the way I had prayed? Was faith missing from my prayers? Why had God failed to fulfill His promises?

As it turned out, I was at fault. Joel and I had had no contact with the outside world and we had lost count of the days. Jules failed to show up on what I thought was Friday evening, when it actually was only a Thursday evening. I tried not to regret it since I had made good use of the time. I had spent the day in prayer and preparation for ending my 36 days of bush life. No wonder when Jules came on Friday and requested me to keep on praying, I felt discouraged. I was surprised that he would encourage me to go on praying when we should have received an answer to our prayer. Things cleared up once he corrected my miscalculations. He reoriented me to the fact that this was Friday and the deadline was Saturday, which was the next day.

I thanked the Lord even in my discouragement that He did not forsake me. I was glad to learn that we still had an extra day until Saturday and deliverance was still in the future. I still had time to rededicate my life to God before leaving the bush.

After Jules had helped me regain a sense of time, I was so happy that I felt as if I was delivered already. I praised the Lord and from that time onwards I decided to go on praying. The miracle I was expecting to happen should be on Saturday I reasoned. Henceforth, I thanked the Lord because I was sure he was going to answer my prayers by sunset. As Saturday unfolded, I was expecting at any minute something miraculous would happen. Whatever it was, I would take it. I was ready.

"Was God going to send an angel to whisk me away to some destination where I would preach about His love?" I wondered. "How would God do it."?

I watched the sun sink into the west. I sat intently hoping something dramatic would happen but soon the sun disappeared without any miracle occurring.

Jules, Joel, and I knelt and prayed together. Words were few. I knew we had done all we could. We had expressed our faith in God. I asked the Lord to make me accept His will in my life. All fear was gone. I asked God to show me what I was to do next.

Farewell to Bush Life

13

This was the final day—Saturday June 6, the day we had given God to perform a miracle or find us another place to go. Joel and I were in the middle of another prayer session when it began to rain heavily. I was completely tired of bush life and the rain actually strengthened my resolve to leave this miserable type of existence. I prayed again: "Lord you are a God who promises and fulfills what you promise. I have talked to you during this entire week and am sure you have heard my prayers. I await your answer. I don't want to stay in this rain any longer. From here I will not go to any other bush or hiding place again. Show me the way I have to take. Amen."

I told my companion to follow me. Finally, I was determined to say goodbye to bush life. I tried to run as much as I could but it was difficult because I was very weak. I was ready to face whatever the world outside was about to give. We arrived at Mr. Kalisa's home but decided not to knock but to make ourselves comfortable under the verandah of one of his houses. It was very dark and nobody could easily see us. I prayed for God's protection.

Immediately, I saw somebody cautiously approach Mr. Kalisa's home with an umbrella in hand. I feared that he might be one of the militias. Since it was dark, the individual could not see us and we remained out of his sight. After announcing his presence, Mr. Kalisa opened the door; I recognized that it was Jules' father from his voice. I could overhear the conversation from where we were and since they did not suspect that anyone was listening, they did not attempt to conceal their conversation.

"Why are you still here?" Jules' father asked Mr. Kalisa.

"Why, is something going on?" Mr. Kalisa responded.

"Yes, everyone has left their homes and have escaped," he continued, "My family and I have also fled. The Rwanda Patriotic Front is approaching"

I could not believe what I was hearing. Could this be God's answer to my prayer?

Unable to contain my excitement, I went and knocked at the door as the two continued to talk.

"Are you still alive?" Mr. Kalisa asked as he opened the door and looked at me in surprise.

This man had been very kind to me. Several weeks had elapsed since I was last at his home and during the time I was hiding in the bush, Jules had told me how Mr. Kalisa's wife had become ill and had died leaving an infant behind. He was now caring for the baby. He was very happy to see us alive, so was Jules' father.

"My son your God has been victorious!" he whispered.

He told me that everybody had fled because of news that the army was now in the area.

"Your friend Jules is at home," he remarked.

"Jules didn't flee with us," he continued. "He stayed behind with some children. He said that there is no better refuge than God so he chose to stay at home."

"Go, join your friend and I know that the God you worship will be with you".

I thanked the Lord for making my friend's father realize that in God was protection. I wish I had spent more time with him to share how God had been with us throughout the difficult times, but this was not possible. Unbeknown to us, in a few days we would be separated forever in this life. I believe it won't be long before we see each other again when Jesus comes. At that time there will be no more Hutus or Tutsis. Jules' father completed his life's journey and now awaits the call of the life-giver when the dead will spring out of their graves never more to die.

Jules' father was not the only one. Many like him are resting in their graves. Those who loved Jesus but died before the genocide know nothing about what happened to us during the tragedy. Many innocent Hutus and Tutsis were killed during the genocide. Some were killed on their knees praying after being granted time to say their last prayers. Others were shot trying to save their lives. Most died from malaria unable to get treatment. Still many died in the Congo Forests as refugees and were buried in shallow graves. Others surrendered themselves to the militias. Mothers abandoned their infants as they tried to escape for their lives, but mostly in vain. Bullets were scattered everywhere and people groped for life. Many collapsed from starvation and exhaustion running for many days with nothing to eat or drink. Some simply sat down and waited for their death.

I will never forget the death of a girl who had been kind to me. During the time I was hiding in the bush, she had brought me food and when I was not able to swallow any food because of the wounds in my throat, she had brought me milk. I remember and will never forget the message she sent me one night after hearing that I had been asked to dig my own grave but was not killed. When she brought me milk, she told me that it was great that had I survived being killed by the militiamen who happened to have been her neighbors.

"The Lord has a work for you to accomplish in your life," she said. "Be sure to preach the good news of salvation until Jesus comes."

I bitterly mourned her death. Whenever I remember her words I am reminded that God spared my life for a special purpose—to preach the good new of salvation through Jesus Christ.

After being told that Jules had remained at home, I decided to go and see him. Before going, I prayed and asked the Lord to give me a sign that He was the one still directing all events in my life. I told God that if He was still leading me, He should not let me meet anybody along the way to Jules' home and that I should go directly into the kitchen where I should meet only one person. If God would make things go this way I would take this for a sign that He was still with me. On the way I did not meet anybody. When I reached Jules' home, I went straight to the kitchen and found one child seated near the fire. God had answered my prayer by granting me the sign I had requested.

When the boy saw me he became afraid and tried to run away. I reassured him that all was well.

I stayed at Jules' home from that time on. My health began to improve. I could eat and sleep. No more mosquitoes! I was, however, told to never go outside the house during the day because several groups of militias were still roaming the neighborhood and could come and kill me at any time. Occasionally, I could hear people speaking outside the house but could never stand up to see who they were. I had to spend the whole day lying down. During the evening I would stretch myself.

I was glad to be in a house after a long time of life in the bush. I spent some time remembering all that I had gone through. I wrote all the dates and events to make sure I would not forget what God had done for me. I also reminded myself of my vows to God.

Within a few days we heard that the entire region was under the control of the Inkotanyi Army (Rwanda Patriotic Front). They were said to be rescuing survivors while hunting down and rounding up all the militias responsible for the killings. Yet we had never seen any soldiers in our vicinity. As far as we were concerned militias were still there. We were told that most of the militias had fled and that others had come back to take their valuables. There was so much confusion. Was the war coming to an end?

Assured that the situation was improving, I went out to stretch and bask in the sun. Unfortunately, when I tried to eat, instead of gaining strength I developed edema.

Jules checked with neighbors what was happening and was told that people had been ordered by the army to leave their homes and gather in a given place. For the whole week word went around asking all to leave their

Farewell To Bush Life   **143**

homes for designated places of safety. I could not join others so I stayed in the house hoping I would soon recover. Meanwhile, all that refused to comply with the order were considered enemies. Those that had been involved in the killings ran away fearing that people would identify them at the gathering. We did not know that our security was tied to this military order.

Jules was very active informing all Tutsis who were in hiding that the army (RPF) had come. Day after day Jules would go searching for survivors, getting them from their hiding places, accompanying them to where the soldiers had asked all people to assemble. From Jules' home I could see people stream along the road, carrying their belongings on their heads. This went on for almost an entire week.

I asked Jules' brother to accompany me on a walk since I was still very weak. This time the road seemed empty. We thought everybody was gone. Suddenly, we saw a multitude numbering thousands, walking in a single file with everyone carrying their own luggage. We could recognize some former businessmen and government officials who were forced to walk while carrying their belongings like common citizens. Some quipped that this was a deliberate way to teach the Rwandese that they were all equal with none more superior to the other. Indeed the ground had been leveled. The rich and the poor, the educated and the uneducated, the Hutu and a few

Tutsi survivors, were all walking. Those that were too sick to walk were pushed in wheel burrows.

Seeing the exodus, we realized that we had overlooked an order that could mean a difference between life and death. We then decided to go back to Jules' home, pick up our belongings and join the group. Jules' brother recommended that we use an alternative road to avoid any danger. We had hardly walked a mile when Jules' brother told me that he had seen a soldier. He told me to run and follow him but I couldn't. Before he could get anywhere, one of the soldiers spotted us and came running ready to shoot. I thought that this was the end of my life. As I threw my hands in the air, my walking stick fell and I struggled to keep my balance. Previously when I sensed that I could die or be killed any moment, I had some time to pray but now my prayer was very brief.

"Lord save me!" I intoned.

God answered my prayer. Instead of immediately shooting me, he decided to capture me alive for; he thought I was one of the militias who had refused to go where everyone had been ordered to go.

"You deserve to die," he screamed.

I showed him my Tutsi ID card, the same card that had gotten me in lots of trouble with Hutu militias throughout the genocide. He refused to believe that I was Tutsi saying that his superiors would not accept that I was truly a Tutsi. And even if I was, I must have been a sympathizer of the militias. I begged him to let me go. But he told me that it was not possible.

As we proceeded to where the commander was, the soldier advised me to tell any lies that could help me escape. I refused. I decided to pray instead. I asked the Lord to be with me and to let His will be done. When I came to where the commander was, I was ordered to sit down. I could tell that his attention was divided. The commander was attracted by what seemed to be a bottle of beer. The commander was busy with other things and I sat there forgotten. After a long time he looked at me with fury in his eyes.

"Who are you?" he asked. "How did you get here?"

I pulled out my ID card and handed it over to him. I told him that I was going to the home of the family that had hidden me. But his attention was still divided. The commander considered sending me to the same soldier who had brought me there, but since this soldier was now in trouble for drinking while on duty, the commander asked me to standby. Turning to me once more, the commander slapped me on my right cheek. I felt the pain but it was nothing in comparison to what I had anticipated. He told me to immediately go to the nearest camp. I went to the first camp and was glad to meet Jules among those that had come earlier.

In the camp I met many Christians who had known me as a preacher. My friend Paul was there also. We were

overjoyed and for a moment we forgot our plight. Every
Saturday at the camp we were granted permission to worship. We discovered that there were so many Christians in
the camp. Some were pastors, church elders, and others
deacons of their respective churches and this made it easy
for us to organize well-structured church services under
the trees. Our camp was not the only one with worship
services. I heard that at Byumba 80 kilometers North of
Kigali, other Christians were also having worship every
Saturday.

After some three or four weeks, everybody was told to
go back to their respective homes. Those that still had
homes to return to went back immediately, but those
whose homes had been destroyed remained in the camp
for some time. There was so much commotion. There
were many children without parents, many men without
wives, and many women without husbands. Many did not
have a home to go to anymore.

For me the most important thing was to find my family
members. I was in Ntongwe 100 kilometers from home.
My family was very big and I had heard that they had
scattered. Where was I to begin? I decided to go back to
Kigali and then go home to Kibuye. I wanted to find out if
my parents and relatives had survived.

Going to Kigali was not easy. I had no money and
transport was scarce. There were only a few military
trucks and a few cars for transportation. My friend Jules

agreed to accompany me on foot to Ruhango and later to Kigali. Memories of brutal killings in Kigali haunted me. Who had been killed and who had escaped? Was there a church or any church member left? These were some of the questions that crossed my mind as I traveled back to Kigali.

Loving My Enemies

14

When I reached Kigali from Ntongwe the first person I met was an elder of a local church I used to attend before the genocide. I was pleased to realize that some people had survived the killing. Since we come from the same village, I hoped he would inform me how my family had fared during the genocide. But he too knew nothing about the situation back home. He asked me to accompany him to a church meeting. The believers I met at the church were so different. Those who had food or clothes freely shared with those who did not have. I was thankful to be a beneficiary of such love as I was given a pair of trousers, shoes, kitchen utensils, and some cash.

I still wanted to know what had become of my family back home. As I was preparing to visit my village, I met Mr. Kagabo who told me what had happened.

"Nobody in your family survived," he told me.

I was shocked. He reiterated that all had been killed. My parents, my seven siblings, nephews, cousins, aunts, and uncles were no more. He went on to tell me how most of the neighbors close to our home had also been killed.

This man went on to explain about my sister Athaly's death. I was greatly pained to learn of how she suffered. She was well known in our village for her kindness. In fact, neighbors had given her many affectionate nicknames because of her generosity. She gave food and clothes to the poor. This man had tried to hide her in his house when many people were being killed. On several occasions the militias would come on their killing spree. At one time this man was in trouble for hiding my sister. She came out of the house and declared: "Let anyone who has anything against me step out and kill me." No one was willing to take her life. The militias recognized who she was and would not dare touch her. They all walked away.

I understand that a few days later, the militias asked an irrational man to kill my sister since they could not do it themselves. He came and cut her to pieces, without any pity.

The man told me of how our village lay in ruins. I wondered why God would spare my life to live in a world where I would not have any relative. Here I was at 24 orphaned and with no relative to commiserate with. Why had God allowed this to happen to me? Why did he not let me die? There was no meaning in my being alive. All my nephews who were age mates were gone. Words could never express my sense of loss. I felt alone. I was alone.

I decided not to go home. I found some comfort in listening to many that had experienced similar losses. I found some escape in accepting preaching appointments where I could testify how God had, miracle after miracle, saved me throughout the genocide. I began to preach all over the country and conducted evangelistic efforts. I tried to avoid going to preach in my own region let alone my own village. I was still grieving for my family that had been wiped out of existence. Besides, I figured that it would be unsafe to go home since one could still be killed. I also heard that every time a survivor went there, the remaining villagers would flee fearing revenge. Many were guilty of having taken cows that belonged to Tutsis and feared they would be asked to pay back. For these reasons, I delayed my going home.

I concluded another evangelistic effort at a place where a church had been destroyed and people had been killed. I planned to go and see a place where one man had managed to hide one hundred people, including a president of our church.

Somehow plans changed. I decided to go to Kibuye first. When I arrived home, I found nobody. Not a single child had survived. They had all been killed. The following morning I met the only survivor from a family that lived close to my sister's house. A soldier who was her brother's friend had protected this girl. The soldier had come to the home of the girl to rescue his friend. When he arrived his friend had just been killed and the soldier offered to protect the girl in place of her brother who had been killed. Since the soldier had found militias killing everybody in that village, he asked them to sell this girl alive to him. They had agreed. He gave them money and he took the girl with him. On their way the soldier told the girl why he had bought her. He told the girl that he would ensure her safety on account of the friendship he had had with her brother who had been killed. The news about what had happened spread quickly and the soldier was imprisoned. The girl went into hiding until the genocide was over.

This is the girl who gave me details of how my family died since she had witnessed the killings. She informed me that my nephews and nieces were killed inside the nearby Catholic Church. She described how one of my nephews who had been badly injured managed to escape. But since he was bleeding profusely, the militias followed the trail of his blood and eventually found and killed him. Two of my other relatives died at the same church after the soldiers had thrown grenades into the church.

I was shown the hill on which machine guns had been mounted to make sure that anybody that would escape from the church would be gunned down. As I listened to details of my family's death, I was enraged beyond words. I decided that going back to Kigali would calm me down. I left my village still haunted by the suffering my family had gone through.

While in Kigali, I reflected on how God had rescued me from critical situations. God had saved me for a purpose! With this conviction, I was ready to consider a request the president of our Mission had made earlier. I accepted the appointment to be the Youth and Education Director of our Mission. My responsibilities included visiting more than 250 churches in the whole Mission. Knowing that God had saved me in an extraordinary way, I was determined to serve Him in an extraordinary way. I embarked on my assignment trusting in God for guidance. I followed a tight itinerary that took me away from Kigali for two months at times. I enjoyed my work. I was thrilled to see people accept Jesus.

In spite of my success, one thought haunted me. "Go back to your region and your village and preach to the people there." These words kept on ringing in my conscience. I then remembered the promise I had made to

God before the genocide. I had pledged that as soon as I got employed, I would use my first salary to preach to my neighbors in my home village. Up till now, I had not fulfilled my vow. My miraculous deliverance during the genocide compounded my guilt.

On several occasions I took refuge in the fact that I was already doing something for God. Even though I had not yet preached in my own village, I was preaching elsewhere. I reasoned that when I made the promise then, my family had been still alive. I had primarily intended to preach to them. But now they were no more. Apart from the unsafe security situation, I reasoned that no one would listen to me. Tension was high and the spirit of revenge was rife. How could they listen to a Tutsi preacher with so many Tutsi skulls still littered on every valley and hill? I was faced with a difficult challenge but I needed to do something to fulfill my promise to God.

I decided to go and preach to the people who had killed my parents, my only brother, my six sisters, and my relatives. As soon as I reached this decision, I informed my fellow pastors and church members of my intentions.

There was stiff resistance. Most of my friends found it absurd that I wanted take the news of salvation to people who had killed my own relatives. Some of my relatives had died without being Christian and chances were that they would not gain eternal life. Here I was planning to go and preach to the militias, giving them a chance to obtain eternal life. Where was the fairness? Wasn't God expecting too much from a mortal?

These issues kept my mind racing through some texts in the Bible that talk of God's unconditional love for His children. If God forgives the vilest of sinners, why could I not reflect such a spirit? Why would "amazing grace" be so amazing if it didn't accomplish the incredible?

Nobody could dissuade me from going back to my village to preach to my "enemies." The people of my village were God's children who needed His mercy and forgiveness. They needed salvation the one thing only God can offer. I was going to preach and leave the results with God. I devoted one week to prayer. I entreated the Holy Spirit to do His part and I would do mine. After all, mine was to pay my vow! I felt compelled to fulfill a promise I had made to God, to preach in my village. With time, I drummed up support for my mission. The pastor assigned to my village arranged everything I needed for the evangelistic meetings I intended to hold.

As the day drew closer, I packed my clothes, books, sermons and microphones. I arrived at my village on Friday evening. Early Saturday morning, Bible in hand, I invited people to come to Church to listen to the word of God. The meetings started that Saturday afternoon. Many were afraid and thought I was after revenge, but I told them to forget the past.

After visiting as many homes as I could, I went to the church. I was encouraged to see many people respond to the invitation. The Lord had brought them there. The local church pastor introduced me and gave me time to greet the people. I told them that I had come to pay my vows to God. I told them how I wished my relatives were alive to hear me speak the word of God, but since they were all gone I still had to come and fulfill what I had promised God before the genocide broke out. I added that God had a plan for their lives that is why He had given them a chance to live. I told them that my prayer was that they would not hear the young man they had known before, but to see in me a messenger of the Almighty God.

I outlined how the evangelistic effort was to proceed. We were not going to hold the meetings at the church. Instead, our venue was a nearby village because of its strategic position. The pastor encouraged the church members to invite as many people as they could to the meetings. Word of invitation spread throughout the entire district. Initially, only children and women came to the meetings. However, on the second day a few men also joined. I was encouraged to learn that some of those who had been leaders in genocide were also coming to the meetings.

Night after night, for eight days many people streamed to hear me preach. At the end of the evangelistic effort, I invited people to give themselves to Jesus. 120 people accepted Jesus as their personal Savior and were subsequently baptized. Praise God!

Among the converts was a man who had killed my sister. I gave him a Bible for a present. I praised God that He had empowered me to do the unimaginable. I don't deserve any credit for what took place. I was glad that God had spoken through me to His children. My heart was at peace because I had paid my vow.

Picking the Broken Pieces

15

Although the genocide shattered the humanity of the people of Rwanda drastically; I found that preaching about salvation and touching on themes such as God's love, forgiveness, and justice was an effective way of starting the healing process in Rwanda. After preaching in my own village, I decided to expand my evangelistic efforts. People were very receptive to the preaching of the gospel and I was going to take advantage of this opportunity to reach out to as many people as I could.

I decided to hold another evangelistic meeting in the Rubengera open-air market in Mabanza Commune, in the city of Kibuye. I already had a strategy in place. I was going to use many large speakers to ensure that as many people as possible could hear me preach. I targeted the two districts that were close to the open-air market. I consulted the pastor responsible for the two districts and he pledged his full support. All the church members in the area were mobilized to invite their friends and relatives to the meetings. I also had enlisted the support of the youth to assist with follow-up work. Choirs from surrounding churches were to be invited to sing at the meetings. We anticipated unity to emerge as people worked side by side in inviting their neighbors to the meetings.

With all these plans afoot, only one problem still remained. We needed permission to preach in the market. Earlier one of the local pastors had applied for permission to use the market grounds for meetings, but the application had been declined on grounds of security. Authorities felt that holding meetings at the market would disrupt the activities at the market.

In one corner of the market I had spotted a place that I considered suitable for the meetings. This was the place they used to sell goats. Usually by lunchtime all goats were sold out and so we could hold our meetings in the afternoon.

I approached the *Bourgoumestre* (Governor) for permission to hold evangelistic meetings in the market. In an attempt to discourage me, he quoted an exorbitant 30,000 Frw for the use of the space. I negotiated and he came down to 20,000 Frw and then down to 10,000 Frw.

"If you can't pay this amount please go out of my office," he said with a degree of impatience. "I can't help you any more!"

I assured him that I would pay the money although I knew I didn't have that sum. I informed the Governor that I would to be back with the money. I left his office praying for a miracle. I then went to our church where I met one of the elders. I told him of the need for rent and he immediately offered me all the money we needed to rent the market for the meetings.

On Saturday afternoon instead of going home, our church members converged at the market to hold further meetings with traders at the market. As I started to preach, many people came to listen to the Word. I prayed that the Lord would empower me with his Spirit so that I could speak without any fear. The Lord answered my prayer. Instead of the numbers decreasing, people increased daily. It seemed that the whole city had stopped to listen to what was going on.

After three days the devil seemed determined to disturb the meetings. One man in the crowd was pretending to be in charge of security of the city. He interrupted my preaching saying that he wanted to address the people. He wanted to take advantage of our meetings to speak to the people. He admitted that he had failed to attract people to his meetings on security matters. I refused him the privilege. I asked him to call for a separate meeting than disturb our meetings. I did not want anybody to dilute God's message that I was preaching.

A group of Muslims also came wanting to talk to the people and they accused me of misleading people. I requested some elders to deal with the problem. I became aware that Satan was not happy to see people surrender their lives to Jesus. The Lord prevented further disruptions of the meetings and there was calm.

One man came forward when I made a call for repentance. He then asked me for an opportunity to give a testimony. I agreed thinking that it was an ordinary testimony. The first part of his testimony was positive. He told of how he had been touched by the messages that were being preached. Then suddenly, he began to deviate.

"I am wondering why people are not coming to the front the way I did," he said. "People need to repent. I can identify many of you here who were involved in the killing during the genocide. I am looking at some of you right now. Surrender yourselves to Jesus like I have done!"

As soon as I realized that his speech could prevent people from coming to the meetings, I promptly yet carefully stopped him. I wanted people to continue coming. I wanted people to hear the word of God so that they could repent without intimidation.

What was obvious during that man's short testimony was that he had been through a lot. He had seen people killed during the genocide and sounded quite traumatized.

Since our meeting was conducted soon after the genocide, most militiamen were not yet rounded up. His impatience was understandable. But our purpose was not to polarize people but to provide one alternative through which healing could begin.

God, however, blessed our meetings. At the end, hundreds had given their lives to Jesus and had decided to be baptized. The week had passed very fast for us. I preached my last sermon. Many wept at the prospect of parting with friends and relatives. We all dispersed resolute on continuing to share the word of God with as many people as we could.

Choosing to Die With the People of Rwanda 16

R oy was an extraordinary missionary who worked
for a church organization in Rwanda when the
genocide broke out. Roy stands out in my mind
because when appeals were made for all expatriates to
leave the country, he chose to stay behind. He was determined to die saving as many people as he could.

After our country's tragedy, the president of Roy's
church visited Rwanda after the genocide. Unfortunately
the president of our country was not able to meet him because of other commitments, but he sent some high-
ranking government officials to represent him. I, together
with other church leaders of our church, had the unique
honor of being present at that meeting. Roy was there too.

I will never forget the words that the key representative from the Rwanda government spoke during the meeting.

"If all Christians in Rwanda had been like Roy, what happened in Rwanda might not have happened," he said.

"I saw Roy, a white man, during the most dangerous moments of the conflict in our country, running between the opposing forces saving the wounded, searching for those who were hidden and bringing them to safety," he continued.

"This man could have been killed, because he was definitely on harm's way. But God showed him that He is always with those that selflessly serve him," He concluded.

The testimony from the government official was not solitary. There are many in Rwanda today that still remember Roy with fond memories. One example is a woman who told me how Roy had helped her during the genocide. This was a woman whom together with her son had been hidden for days by a Hutu pastor. When the pastor heard that the Rwanda Patriotic Front Army was fast approaching, the pastor decided to flee. But before he could do so he prayed asking God to protect the woman. No sooner had the pastor left than Roy came and took the mother and her child to safety.

Another incident that I will never forget is that which took place in my village at Kicukiro. This incident provides a point of contrast between Roy's sacrificial com-

mitment to the people of Rwanda as opposed to an international army that stood by as people were killed. In
Kicukiro was a large military base for the United Nations
Army Mission in Rwanda (UNAMIR). When the genocide started, over three thousand civilians fled to this
army base for refuge. When the militias heard that civilians were seeking protection from the United Nations
Army they went and demanded the release of the Tutsis
into their hands.

Since the United Nations Army had not been given any
directive to intervene in the genocide, they pulled out of
Kicukiro leaving the Tutsis at the mercy of the militias.
Before the United Nations Army could leave, however,
people pleaded with the United Nations Army to shoot
them instead of leaving them to fall prey to the machetes
of the ruthless militias. Many Tutsis lay in the roads,
blocking the way of the United Nations Army tankers. To
disperse the crowds the United Nations Army fired some
shots in the air. The militias killed over 3000 defenseless
civilians while the United Nations Army literally waved
goodbye. But Roy, without any army was committed to
die trying to save as many people as he could.

Although I had known Roy before the genocide, our
relationship strengthened after the genocide had come to
an end when we worked closely to preach the good news
of salvation in Jesus Christ. We were glad to be part of a

process towards ethnic reconciliation that Rwanda was beginning to experience.

When I returned to Kibuye my home city, I decided to go back to school to further my education. Roy visited me and together we organized large evangelistic efforts together. He was very resourceful for he donated microphones that were used in my preaching ministry. He also provided our pastors with bicycles to alleviate their transport problems.

One thing that impressed me about Roy was his willingness to identify with people. I recall Roy coming to my humble dormitory room to advise me on plans for evangelism. Earlier, when I was in Kibuye, I remember him traveling a great distance by motorcycle to come and participate in an evangelistic effort. Under harsh conditions he was prepared to stay with us in spite of his high position.

On one occasion, I was planing to run another evangelistic effort in Kigali. I did not have any money to fund such a big project. I consulted with my Mission president and he tried to get authorization to hold the meeting in the city. Unfortunately, the request was turned down. I spent the whole day running from place to place trying to get someone to mediate on my behalf. I met Roy in the morning before meeting my Mission president. When I met him later in the day I told him about our failure to get authorization for a meeting. Roy told me that he knew the mayor of Kigali very well. He had become acquainted with her during the genocide when Roy was busy rescuing hunted people. At that time the mayor of Kigali was one of the majors in the Rwanda Patriotic Front Army. He would try to intervene.

The next day Roy took me to the prefecture to obtain authorization for the evangelistic meetings. We were not able to see the mayor that morning because he was busy. Roy assured me that he would come back later to see him. So we went our separate ways.

I went to the Union Headquarters where I met a gentleman who called me by name yet we had never met before.

"Are you Phodidas?" he asked.

"Yes!" I replied.

"How is the youth program coming?" he inquired.

"It's all fine," I said. "We are busy making arrangements for several big meetings with the youth."

"I believe you need some money for the meetings," he said.

"Yes, we do!" I responded in amazement.

"How much money do you need?" he further asked.

"Enough to purchase 200 Bibles for the first meeting," I said.

"Anything else?" he asked.

"We also need money for the transportation of singers to the meetings," I told him.

He then asked me to give him a detailed list of all the things we needed and assured me that he would provide the money. As I discovered later, this gentleman was the director of the Church Ministries Department based in our Church Headquarters in Abijan, Ivory Coast. Later, I learned that Roy had talked to this man the night before and had informed him of our plans to conduct a massive preaching meeting in Kigali and our limited funds for the project. God had answered our prayer. The financial obstacle was now out of the way.

It was now 11.00 o'clock in the morning on Friday, the last day before the meetings were scheduled to begin. All churches in Kigali had been informed where to go the following Saturday. Many visitors had been invited and more than 24 choirs were to participate in the program. Only a few people knew of the problems that we were faced with. Those who were aware of the hitches were praying for a miracle. Roy was still trying to negotiate for authorization and I waited outside the offices praying.

I understood the immensity of the problem because earlier one secretary had indicated that cases like ours needed a few days to process and to ascertain the availability of security for the size of crowd we hoped to attract. But I was somehow confident that God was with us and that something would be worked out. At sunset, I saw Roy coming. He was smiling and I knew that we had been authorized to hold the meetings. Our God had worked a miracle! Roy handed me the letter authorizing us to conduct the meetings. The church members in Kigali were overjoyed to learn that our request had been granted.

The following day, Kigali was a hive of activity as cars, buses, and taxis streamed to the Muhima district. Seventh-day Adventist believers came from more than 20 churches in Kigali. There were many Adventist Youth groups in uniform who directed people to the place where the meetings were to be held.

The city was surprised by what was going on. All Seventh-day Adventists were now united in one mission, modeling unity in the aftermath of genocide. We managed to conduct a total of 42 evangelistic efforts and Kigali would never be the same again. During the first baptism, 640 people were baptized.

Much of what people know about Rwanda is the genocide but little is said about the revival that followed. There was a remarkable spirit of cooperation between Hutus and Tutsis as they worked for God. Many organized evangelistic efforts going back to their own villages despite the fact that for most people their entire families had been killed or imprisoned.

The president of our church together with other church leaders in Rwanda wrote letters to all the churches appealing for unity and reconciliation. Most of these leaders had experienced indescribable loss during the genocide but worked hard to bring all people together.

Preaching the good news of salvation did not exclude those that had been imprisoned. The name of James comes to mind. He is one of the wealthy church members who converted his truck into a mobile baptistery. We went from prison to prison preaching to many that are accused of participating in the killings during the genocide. The prisoners who could not attend evangelistic meetings were now being evangelized in prison.

Throughout the country, thousands were surrendering their lives to Jesus. In many areas, civil authorities that gave us permission to preach to the prisoners also came to witness what was happening. The Holy Spirit touched many hearts of the accused killers and they repented publicly. As a result the relatives of those they killed forgave some killers.

Pray for Rwanda. My people and my country went through a lot. In as much as what happened in Rwanda is beyond wildest imagination, the miracles that God did for other survivors and myself are also beyond wildest imagination. Your prayers for healing will be appreciated.

To order more copies of this book do any one of the following:

1. Search the title: *Rwanda, Beyond Wildest Imagination* on Amazon.com and place your order.

2. Ask for the book in any Bookstore near you; if not in stock ask them to order it for you.

3. Send a check or money order of $12.99 + $2.00 shipping and handling to: Lesley Books, 308 Park Avenue, Berrien Springs MI 49103, USA.

Other books by the same author include:
1. *Leading the Leader* a book on how to successfully relate with manipulative subordinates.
2. *Racing Against Time* a book on how to deal with terminal illness.